SNAPSHOTS
OF A LIFE

SNAPSHOTS OF A LIFE

A nonagenarian's recollections
of a North-East childhood,
the Fleet Air Arm, industry
and the stage

BOB WALTON

First published in paperback in 2017 by Sixth Element Publishing
on behalf of Bob Walton

Sixth Element Publishing
Arthur Robinson House
13-14 The Green
Billingham
Stockton on Tees
TS23 1EU
Tel: 01642 360253
www.6epublishing.net

ISBN 978-1-908299-98-7

British Library Cataloguing in Publication Data. A catalogue record for this
book is available from the British Library.

Bob Walton asserts the moral right to be identified as the author of this work.

Printed in Great Britain.

Cover photo: Bob Walton on Ryhope Beach, 1949

Bob Walton at Christmas 2016

CONTENTS

INTRODUCTION

This memoir was begun after a remark by my friend Stan Burnicle (of whom much more later) as we sat together one afternoon sipping whisky and recalling old times. After hearing some of my recollections, he said: "Why don't you write a book, Bob?" I had never thought of such a thing. Later that same day, my wife said: "You know Bob, you ought to do it. Over the years you've related your experiences to your children, your grandson, your fellow Rotarians and others, but now that your two granddaughters and new grandson are in South Africa they may not realise where they come from".

I was born between the two world wars and raised on tales of war in the trenches, and was later myself actively involved during the second conflict. To understand just what it was like for a young person growing up between the wars, it is necessary to have some background information: about the living conditions, and also about the lower expectations in life. For some school leavers (aged fourteen back then), their only aim was to have a job that brought in a wage packet to support their family. I remember a young friend of mine being asked what he wanted to do on leaving school. He replied: "Go down the digger". That meant the coal mine at Ryhope, for he wished to follow in the footsteps of his father or elder brothers. To some youngsters this was the natural path to take. The County of Durham had major coal deposits, and numerous coalmines dotted the county. So more opportunities seemed to be available in this industry than in any other.

It was not an ideal world: leaving school at fourteen, then trying to find employment in an overcrowded labour market, besides living in a world still recovering from a terrible conflict. There was social deprivation and mass unemployment. Social security payments, benefits and labour laws such as we have today to help cushion the blow of redundancy were non-existent. There may have been some help from the "parish" as it was called, but if there was a worker in the household, then payments were often refused. In any case, the family might only have been issued with vouchers to go to the Co-op or some such store to obtain goods in return. It is therefore understandable that occasional unrest occurred among the population. The miners were not treated with a great deal of kindness by the mine-owners, and this was one reason for the bitter strikes of the 1920s and '30s. Those were the conditions for any young person growing up. Yet to us it all seemed natural at the time. It is only on reflection, and upon comparing it with today's lifestyle, that it seems to have been full of hardship. Yet it was also a time when things were beginning to change. More attention was being paid to improving living conditions and housing and the provision of essential services such as gas, electricity, and collecting household waste.

Although I was too young to fully appreciate the political events I saw, or to understand other changes taking place, I will here endeavour to describe them, along with what it meant to a young person growing up in a country where the school map showed the Union Jack over a large part of the globe, while here in the mother country many families were living in poor housing, often without running water, without electricity or even an indoor toilet. I will also try to recall many of the events in my life, both amusing and not so amusing, including my short spell in the Royal Navy, my demobilisation in 1947, and my entry into the world of the working man.

FAMILY BACKGROUND

I was born on Sunday, 6 March 1927 in a terraced council house in Williams Terrace, opposite the cemetery in Ryhope in County Durham. These were houses that had been built shortly after the Great War. I was to learn later that my future parents-in-law had also begun their married life near there. I was the last of five children, two of whom died in infancy. My parents Arthur Walton and Margaret Alice (née Prior) were married in 1910 in Sunderland. Their first child, Alice Ivy, was born in 1912. Olive and Leslie followed, who both died, and then came my sister Doreen in 1922 and myself at the tail-end in 1927.

Mother and father were from reasonably large families. The Priors had four boys and two girls: Harry, George, Ernest, Bob, Alice and Jenny. The Waltons were Bob, Percy, Arthur, Florence and Sally. Both my grandfathers were seafarers, and both were called Bob, but they died before I was born. Since two of my uncles were named Bob, the name obviously runs in the family. I only knew my two grandmothers a short while, for they both died in the 1930s before the Second World War. Grandma Prior lived on her own in an old people's bungalow in Seaham, and Grandma Walton was in Edlington near Doncaster, where she lived with my Aunt Sally. She had moved there with her husband and young son Stanley when the new South Yorkshire coalfields opened, as had many other mining families from the north-east during the Depression. All the time I knew her, my Grandma Walton was totally blind, and my most vivid recollection of her was sitting in her large rocking chair singing the old music hall song "Just a Song at Twilight". Whenever I hear that song, I think of her.

The only other family member who went to sea was my father's younger brother Percy. He was a ship's engineer until late in life, when he and his wife Agnes took over the County Laundry in Newcastle. They had only one child: a son, Alan Hull Walton, who became an author and translator. I always remember visiting

Uncle Percy in Larkspur Terrace in Newcastle because they had a large house with a grand piano in the front room, and an attic that had been converted into a small cinema seating 22 people. Not only that, they had a maid named Betty who had served them since she was a young girl. In a way she was a companion to Alan. I thought they were rich.

My mother's only sister, Jenny, married Bill Duell. He was an engine driver at the docks in Sunderland. They had four sons and two daughters. One of their sons, Alby, entered the army at the beginning of the war and, like many other Wearsiders, was sent to Singapore when the Japanese invaded Malaysia. After the city fell, he was never heard of again.

My father followed the trade of upholsterer and in 1912 was offered a job at the asylum in Ryhope, as it was then called (properly known as Cherry Knowle Hospital). So the family moved to Ryhope and settled into their new community. One aspect of the job I remember was that father was paid once a fortnight; the week with no pay was called "baff" week.

Cherry Knowle Hospital, Ryhope
(courtesy of Philip Curtis, Sunderland Antiquarian Society)

RYHOPE

Farming had been the mainstay of Ryhope until shafts were sunk for coal mining in the mid-eighteenth century. Then it became home to two communities: those who earned their living directly from the production of coal, and those who did not. The mining community was based in the colliery, living in houses built for the miners around the area of the pit. The other section of the population lived around the old village, where three or four farms still existed near the green. At the centre of the green there stood the war memorial, commemorating those who had fallen in the First World War. The use of horses for transportation was still a regular feature, so at the edge of the village green there was a stone horse trough at the point where the road branched off towards Seaham Harbour. There was another trough about 200 yards away, by the turn-off to Silksworth. Even the medical superintendent at the hospital was often seen riding round the village with his family in their pony and trap. There were so many horses that you regularly saw young men going round with barrows, collecting the horse manure lying in the streets and then wheeling it away to spread on their gardens or allotments. It was a valuable commodity in the days when fertilisers were not readily available.

The colliery houses for the miners and their families had been built when public transport was not so common, so they were near enough to the pit for the miners to walk to work. Many rows of colliery houses were not built of brick, but of stone. These dated from the middle to late 19th century. I recall that all of these stone-built houses led directly on to the back street. Their back door in each case was split in two, and you could open up the top half. One would often see the occupants leaning on the bottom half of the door, talking to their neighbours or to passers-by. Some houses were later built of brick, and the street names can still tell you when they were built – such as Mafeking

Terrace, which was built shortly after the Boer War. There was also a street called Brick Row, presumably because it was unusual to use brick as a building material at the time.

Miners and their families were allowed to live in their houses rent-free, and they also received a free monthly allowance of coal. This free coal was delivered by being dumped at the rear of the house near to the coal house in the back yard. It was then shovelled into the coalhouse via a hatch built into the wall, or carried by buckets up the back yard and thrown into the coalhouse through the door. During the early thirties, a time of mass unemployment, it was common to see young men following the coal delivery wagons and offering to shovel in the coal in order to earn sixpence (two-and-a-half pence in today's money).

Of those families who did not directly receive their living from the pit, some worked at the mental hospital or the Co-op, while others travelled to work in the factories or shipyards in Sunderland with their engineering works.

The spread of housing in Ryhope over time brought about a gradual encroachment on the village area. A slow integration of the two communities began to take place. Occasionally one would be awakened on a Sunday morning in the village area by a man making a loud noise with what was like a football supporter's rattle. He would traverse the streets giving his rattle a few turns and shouting in a booming voice: "Pit lies the morn, pit lies the morn. A special meeting will be held in the Miner's Hall", and so on. He was saying that the pit would be idle the next day, and a meeting was to be held to discuss the matter. This was the recognised method of informing the workers so that everyone knew what was going on.

There was also a custom that when a fatality occurred at the pit, it would shut down as a mark of respect for the person killed. And when the burial took place, the funeral procession would be preceded by the colliery brass band playing the "Dead March". The elaborate pit banner, draped in black, would accompany the cortege. Such a sight was not uncommon before the War. It exemplified the close-knit values of the mining community.

The closure of all the coal mines in County Durham in recent years has also meant the loss of most of the colliery brass bands. What a great shame it is that a form of pleasure for many, and a means of passing on musical appreciation and skills to future generations, has been lost, and in most cases might never return. There are some people, however, who have kept the bands alive. One example is our nephew Malcolm Smith, who together with others has been reviving interest in this form of music in Ryhope.

By today's standards, living conditions in the 1920s and early '30s could be described as primitive. I knew of no house in our area that boasted an indoor flush toilet – not even the local doctor, whose practice was in the same street as us. Most toilets were situated in the back yard and were just large, hinged wooden seats fixed to the outside wall. A large hole in the seat led to a space below. It was in this space underneath that the ashes from the coal fires and the rest of the household rubbish was dumped. Each week, the council dust cart went through the streets, and at each house the dustmen would raise the outside covers on the street wall and proceed to shovel all the waste into their wagon. Even today you can visit some of these streets and see where these covers were situated before they were bricked up when modernisation came in the middle-to-late 1930s. Examples of the old coalhouses and toilets can be seen at the Open Air Museum at Beamish in County Durham. The schools were the only exception with regard to toilets. They had flush toilets situated away from the main building, down the school yard.

Not many houses had any indoor plumbing. There was generally an outside water tap in the back yard to serve the household, and buckets of water had to be carried into the house during the day. Things considered essential today, such as central heating and an efficient hot water supply, were non-existent.

Ryhope & Silksworth Co-op
(courtesy of Philip Curtis, Sunderland Antiquarian Society)

The horse and cart still played a large part in the everyday life
of many communities. Horse-drawn vehicles were used by many
traders plying their wares, particularly the various departments
of the Ryhope and Silksworth Co-op, whose carts went out each
day selling goods from its butcher, baker, greengrocer and dairy.
It was amusing to see the horses pulling the milk delivery carts,
proceeding at a walking pace without any instructions from the
driver. They had become so accustomed to the work that they
just ambled along as the dairyman removed milk bottles from
the back of the cart and ran up the path of each house to make
his delivery. Other Co-op carts had their pitches at various points
throughout the area. The local housewives knew their schedules
and would be there to purchase what they needed.

Working wives were in the minority, as most women stayed at
home to look after their families. There was generally a weekly
routine for their housework, for washing, ironing, bread-baking
and so on. Our mothers were always there when we came
home from school. There were no such things as school meals.
Children walked to school in the morning, went back home for

lunch, returned to school for their afternoon lessons, then went back home again at the end of the school day. Many husbands also went home for lunch if they worked not too far away, and if their work routine allowed it. It all meant a busy life for the housewife. Most houses had ranges in the kitchen with coal as the source of heat for cooking and baking bread. Some houses did have gas cookers, but they were in a minority. Baking bread meant making the dough and allowing it to rise in the hearth by the oven, then popping it into the coal-fired oven when it had risen enough. The fire was also the means of heat for the iron when pressing the clothes after the weekly wash. These irons were of solid metal and were placed on the hob or such place near to the fire. They had to be removed carefully when hot, so as not to burn your hands before using them to press the clothes.

Many of the roads were made of cobbles or crushed stone. In a number of areas, the roads were worn down and full of potholes after it rained. Only the major roads were tarmacadamed. Except for the major roads, street lighting was provided by gas. The lamps were placed at intervals along the street and lit each night by the lamplighter, who walked along with a long pole. It had a hook at one end, and he pushed it up through a flap in the base of the lamp, about 10 feet from the ground. The hook engaged with a lever, and when this was pulled down it caused an inrush of gas that was lit by the pilot jet near to the mantle. These street lights were ideal for us youngsters to play under, and they were the only illumination available to us outside when it was not raining, apart from the light provided by the windows of the corner shop.

Gas was also the main source of light in practically every home. The gasman visited regularly to clean and check the lamps in the house, and he would also replace broken or faulty gas mantles. Since there was no electricity in the houses, none of our modern electrical household devices were available back then. Hand-operated carpet sweepers were the norm, and once a year there was a spring clean. Carpets were taken up and draped over lines in the street and beaten severely with carpet beaters. You could see the dust flying all over the place.

By the mid-1930s, the old stone houses were being pulled down, with more modern houses slowly rising in their place. These newer houses had indoor plumbing for toilets and hot water systems for bathing, but of course no central heating yet. That came much later. This renewal of housing had to be discontinued when the Second World War began, and the programme was only completed after the War.

Fire hydrants stood at certain points along the streets. These were made of cast iron and stood about three feet high – thus ideal for young boys to vault over. There was a fire station on Burdon Road. It had a bell on the roof, and when it rang, the firemen (presumably volunteers) rushed to push out the handcart containing their equipment and headed for the scene of the fire. At some point in the mid-1930s, this method of fire-fighting became redundant and was replaced by more efficient motorised units from Sunderland.

Methods of communication were slow by today's standards. Most radios – "wireless sets", as we called them then – worked on batteries or accumulators, and when they started to run down you took them to the accumulator shop where they were recharged. The shop would provide you with a spare until you returned to pick up your own again. Television was in its infancy and regarded as a thing of the future. Not even telephones were a regular feature in the household. Phone boxes were situated at various points throughout the area, but I honestly believe that some people were terrified to use them, they were so new-fangled. I was seventeen before I ever spoke on the telephone at all.

In the back yard of the house in Smith Street, Ryhope, ca 1930

Smith Street, Ryhope, ca 1931

Bob at the photographer's, ca 1932

Bob's first school photo, at the St Paul's
Church of England Infant School, 1933

INFANCY AND SCHOOL DAYS

In my childhood, summer began with the July holidays: it was always warm and sunny, and it ended when we returned to school. Winters were always cold and windy with regular falls of snow to let us slide on the ice and play on our sledges. Kids could play unhindered in the streets, as the only traffic was the occasional slow-moving, horse-drawn tradesman's cart. They were the days when the back streets were criss-crossed with washing lines when the housewives took advantage of a stiff breeze to dry items of washing that were too large for the back yards of their houses. Space was limited there, and large sheets would have rubbed against the walls of the yard.

Back then, we also had seasonal visits from the French onion men. They arrived at the docks in Sunderland, and from there branched out into the district with overladen bicycles going from street to street, door to door, selling that year's crop of onions. It was a familiar sight back then, but not any more.

Those were also the times when one would see men on the coastal roads pushing bikes with sacks of sea coal that they had gathered from the foreshore. This coal would be used to provide fuel for the winter, or be sold to supplement their income and to provide extras for the family. This particular sight was also described by J.B. Priestley in one of his books. It was also a time when we would wake up on a cold winter's morning and scrape the ice off the inside of the bedroom window. We would hear the clip-clop of the milkman's horse slowly moving up the street – with the horse apparently knowing when to move and when to stop, without any command needed from the delivery man. Life certainly moved at a leisurely pace.

Children normally do not remember much before they are 3 years old, so I do not remember my days in Williams Terrace where I was born. And I have but few recollections of my parents' second house in Ryhope, which was in Smith Street. One incident

I do vividly recall was when I was sitting in my high chair having a meal. I was given a plate of cut-up bacon, but it contained a quantity of fat that I decided I disliked, so I pushed it away and declared it to be "kaka". I also remember visits to the house by my Uncle Jim Carter, who regularly called in for a cup of tea and a sandwich before going back to his depot. I can still picture him sitting there eating his cheese sandwiches, hearing him slurp his tea through his big bushy moustache – often as not drinking it from his saucer.

Within a year or so, we moved from Smith Street into a nearby street called Thomas Street, probably because it was a larger house with more living space. It was in Thomas Street that I remember the one and only dog we had: a mongrel called Floss. Unfortunately, we did not have her long before she died, and my father buried her in the back yard where there was a small patch of earth.

It was in Thomas Street that I remember my first encounter of industrial strife. I was standing at the bottom of the street when I saw a group of policemen marching along, with dirty-faced men in the middle of them. They stopped now and again, at which one of the men would emerge and go into a nearby house. Then the group would move on again. These men were called "blacklegs"; they were pitmen who had chosen to work while their comrades were on strike. The strikers did not take too kindly to these strike breakers, whom they also called "scabs". They had to be escorted home by the police, or they would have been attacked by the miners who were on strike. This would have been about 1931 or 1932. The pithead baths did not open until about the mid-1930s, so the strike-breakers were still covered in coal dust when they got home (baths were generally taken in a tin bathtub that would be hung on the back of the kitchen door until required). Twenty or thirty years later, those strike-breakers were still not forgotten. When people spoke of them, they would still be referred to as the "blacklegs".

It was in Thomas Street that I began to acquire my boyhood friends. We all went out in the street to play, as there were no worries about traffic with so few cars on the road. There was one particular friend who lived three or four doors away, Alan Yeaman. His father was an insurance salesman, but also dealt in property, and he owned a car that he used for his business, a "Baby Austin". We two lucky boys would on occasion be allowed to go out with him on his rounds. It really was a treat to ride in a motor car. The only other private car in which I rode belonged to my Uncle Bill and Aunt Jenny (my mother's sister). Uncle Bill was a railway engine driver down at the Sunderland docks, so he had a good wage and was one of the few people able to afford to run a car.

Andrew Banks lived a couple of streets away, at 12 Dinsdale Street. He later joined the Merchant Navy and took part in the North Atlantic convoys. He and his wife Laura still live in the house where he was born and brought up. Another member of our gang of boys was Billy Cook, whose mother was a midwife – though when one boy, Donald Beezer, saw the "County Midwife" plate on their door, he asked: "Is that the County Madwife?" Billy had an uncle who travelled abroad and one day brought him a monkey as a present. A cage was rigged up in a building in the backyard and we boys would go and watch the monkey perform. There was no control on importing live animals in those days.

It was when we lived in Thomas Street that I started school. We were Anglicans, so I was sent to the Church of England school in the village. In earlier days it had been the original church building itself, but had become far too small for the growing community. So when the much larger St Paul's Church was built 300 yards away during the latter half of the 19th century, the old church was converted into a school. There were two other schools in Ryhope. One was St Patrick's, which belonged to the Roman Catholic Church, and the other was the Council School, which was administered by the local authority. Some of the Roman Catholic teachers were nuns who lived in the convent along the Seaham Road. All the children at that school – who included many of our friends – said that those nuns were very strict disciplinarians. My own first teacher at school was Miss Smith; the head teacher was

Miss Maughin (which we all pronounced as "Maffin"). I came across Miss Smith's husband about eighteen years later, as I shall mention in another chapter. There were only three classes in this infant school.

In those days children were given milk at school – one third of a pint – and we drank it just before morning playtime. It wasn't free, but cost one halfpenny a bottle, in other words two pence ha'penny a week. I recall that one Monday morning, when my mother gave me the milk money for the week, it was all in half pennies. I didn't think this was correct, so I refused to take it. I can still remember being in the infants' class near to the outer door leading to the cloakroom when I saw my mother at the classroom door calling to Miss Smith to give her the money. We moved to the church junior school after two years, when we were about seven. It stood directly opposite the entrance to St Paul's Church. We stayed there for two more years before transferring to the Council School. The school rooms in the junior church school were heated by large open coal fires. The morning milk was placed near to them, meaning that those bottles nearer to the fire were lovely and warm when we drank the milk. So in the colder months we would rush to get the warmer bottles to help keep out the chill of the winter.

In about 1935, the boys all transferred to the Council School to be prepared for the grammar school entrance exam, which was sat at the age of eleven. The girls did not transfer to another school, but stayed at the Church of England junior school, where they sat their exams for the girls' grammar school at Seaham. Our classes at the Council School had only boys in each class, and from this time onwards, all my education was in boys-only classes.

The church obviously played a major role in my early years, from schooling to my membership of church organisations. One of the events we eagerly looked forward to each year was the annual Sunday-school picnic. The Sunday schools in the area would all march to the fields near the mental hospital where we were given a bag of goodies containing cakes, sweets and the like, and then we took part in races and other competitions.

We progressed from Sunday school to Bible class, and those of us boys who attended would be invited to the vicarage by Canon Little after evensong on a Sunday. He had served in the First World War as a padre. At the vicarage we played draughts with him, chess, Ludo etc. Other boys would be in the games room of the vicarage playing billiards and other games. Some of us would just listen to the radio, our favourite programme being "Happidrome", a kind of variety show hosted by the three north-country comedians Ramsbottom, Enoch and Harry Korris. The evening at the vicarage was a highly enjoyable boy's club.

By 1935 we had moved to a house in Gray Terrace that had four rooms and a kitchen/pantry, but still no indoor hot water, bathroom or toilet. It was here, in Gray Terrace, that two people entered my life who would have a considerable impact: Mr Phillips and Miss Eales. The first was my piano teacher, the second my elocution teacher. I shall return to them in due course below.

Our final move in Ryhope was to 3 Colin Terrace in about 1937, near to the church schools. A builder called Humble built some houses on empty land belonging to the Anglican church, and my parents decided to buy one. The price was £475 I believe – an insignificant sum today, but at that time probably 150 to 200 times a man's weekly wage. This was the first house my parents ever owned, and the first with indoor, hot and cold running water. There was no central heating, but it had a bathroom and an indoor toilet. Wonderful. 1937 was coronation year, and this was reflected in two street names on our small estate: Coronation Avenue and Marina Terrace – the latter referred to the bride of the Duke of Kent, Princess Marina. Our street was named after the builder's grandson. The only other street on the estate was Floralia Avenue. I do not know the origin of the name.

St Paul's Church and School, Ryhope, early 20th century
(courtesy of Philip Curtis, Sunderland Antiquarian Society)

St Paul's Church, Ryhope
(courtesy of Philip Curtis, Sunderland Antiquarian Society)

1. Robert Walton, 22 Gray Terrace.
2. Joan Christian, 5 Lyndhurst Terrace.
3. Norma Brewster, 9 James Williams St.
4. Dorothy Caslaw, 42 Barnard Street.
5. Brian Greathead, 48 St. Aidan's Ave., Ryhope Road.
6. Kathleen Pears, 21 Mitford Street.
7. Arthur Goldsworthy, 50 Hood Stre
   Jean Pearson, 25 Ridley Terre
   Leslie Charlton, 61 Annie Stre
10. Doreen Hopper, 9 Westfield Grove.
11. Marjorie Robson, 4 Fowler Terrace.
12. Sheila Gowland, 77 Cleveland Road.
13. George Williamson, 2 Hawthorn St.
14. Laurence and Dorothy Wood, Ivy Cottage, Durham Road.
15. Laurence Keenan, 48 Fulwell Road.
16. Frank Plemper, 12 Gilsland Street S.
17. Sheila Wright, 2 Moine Gardens, Roker.
18. Hazel Telford, 28 Western Hill.

Bob's birthday photo in the Sunderland Echo, 1936 (top left)

Bob back at the photographer, 1936

In the garden in Colin Terrace, 1938: Bob (left)
with Alan Yeaman and his younger brother George

SHOPPING IN RYHOPE

I was now at an age when I could do all my mother's messages, and would often be sent off to the Co-op with a shopping list. I would often place the shopping basket over my head, rest it on my shoulders, and walk up the road with my hands free. How many households have shopping baskets today? It's all plastic carriers from the supermarkets. But that was the time when small corner shops were very well patronised, long before the arrival of the supermarket. The shop nearest to us was owned by a family called Storey. Like many others, this family of shopkeepers lived on the premises. They sold everything for your household needs – vegetables, sweets, sugar, tobacco, etc. Much of their stock, like sugar and flour, was stored in large wooden bins. There was not much pre-packed food in those days before the war. Sweets were kept in large glass jars on the counter, and when a youngster went for his sweeties the shopkeeper would dip his hand into the jar, weigh the sweets, then pour them from the pan of the scales into a paper bag.

Mother would say "Go to Storey's and get me two pennyworth of pot stuff". This meant one or two potatoes, a carrot or two, and perhaps a leek so she could make some form of broth. Perhaps it was Dad who wanted me to run an errand. Then it might be: "Bobby, go and get me half an ounce of Brown Jack Twist". This was a kind of pipe tobacco that came in a roll, and the shopkeeper would cut off a section of it, weigh it, put it into a bag and give it to me. If I remember correctly, it cost about three ha'pence. Father would cut off enough from the tobacco to fill his pipe, roll it in his hands, then stuff it into the bowl of the pipe, sit back and enjoy it.

It was customary for each household to have their milk delivered every morning by the roundsman, but if one ran out of milk during the day for some reason, that wasn't a problem. There was a dairy nearby, run as a partnership by Armstrong &

Staples. Mother would give me a jug and tell me to pop over and get a pint of milk. You just had to knock at the house door, since it was attached to the small dairy. Whoever answered the door would take your jug, you followed him into the dairy, and there he would dip the measure into the churn and pour the milk into your jug. If no one was available at the dairy, then all you had to do was go round to the farm at the top of the village and get your milk in the same manner.

There was a chain of stores called "The Meadow Dairy". They sold eggs, butter, sugar and so on. These stores sold the butter loose – in other words, there was a large lump of butter behind the counter that would be taken out of a tub, and when you asked for, say, a pound, the assistant would pick up two wooden butter pats and work off a lump of butter with them. He put it on the scales, adding more or taking something off as required, all with the use of the pats. When the right weight was achieved, then he squared the butter with the pats and wrapped it in the appropriate paper, again all done with the pats. This firm had the motto "We never sell a bad egg". There was a machine in the shop, on top of which were holes into which the assistant placed each egg. Lights under the eggs would show if there was a bad one, as these were more opaque than the good eggs. This store also followed the example of others such as Duncan's (a chain store similar to The Meadow Dairy) in that they took back empty jam jars and gave a ha'penny in return for each.

My parents knew the manageress of The Meadow Dairy, and she would let me go out with the store delivery boy on occasions. His name was Frank Leonard. I did it for the pleasure of it, and to give Frank some company on his rounds. No payment was involved. Frank was three or four years older than me and would be dressed in the Meadow Dairy uniform consisting of a dark green jacket and trousers that tucked into leggings and boots. He also had a peaked cap and a pair of gauntlet gloves to finish it off. He rode a tricycle with a box at the front in which the groceries were carried for delivery. Frank would load up for his daily round, and off we'd go around the streets of Ryhope. One day it started to rain, but the deliveries were just about finished so I climbed into the box at the front for shelter. As we trundled through the streets, I would shout out where we were. Frank asked "How do you know?", so I told him I was looking through the keyhole at the front. At this, he stopped the trike, came to the front and stuffed the keyhole up with paper. Eventually, we got back to the shop and he came to let me out, but couldn't get the key into the lock. It was getting rather stuffy inside, and he was getting worried in case he lost his job. But he finally succeeded to the relief of us both. I never went out with him again.

GRAMMAR SCHOOL

In 1936/37 I sat the examination to secure a place at the local grammar school. There were two exams. The first was at your own school, and if you passed it you had to sit the second in the grammar school itself. In previous years it had been the practice to have a final interview after the second test, but this was discontinued the year before I sat my exams. I was lucky enough to pass both and so was offered a place at the grammar school in Ryhope. As a reward for passing, and also because it was considered an honour to be selected (there were only about 7 or 8 successful boys in total from the whole of Ryhope), my parents bought me my first bicycle: a Raleigh sports model purchased at Palmer's in Sunderland. The price, I seem to recollect, was four pounds, seven shillings and sixpence. That was double the wages of some working men.

The grammar school catered for pupils from Easington, Seaham, Whitburn, Silksworth and Ryhope. It was a privilege to be able to go there, and we were taught algebra, geometry, trigonometry, arithmetic, Latin, French, chemistry, physics, biology and other subjects – a much more comprehensive range of subjects than what we had been taught before. There was also one additional subject that was never offered at the Council School at the time, namely woodwork. Pupils could also look forward to trips to France on entering their third year. Visiting foreign countries wasn't possible for pupils at other schools, but the War meant it wouldn't happen for me either.

Discipline was strict, as it was in all schools back then. We didn't wear ordinary outdoor shoes at school, only sand shoes, and when we entered on a morning we had to change shoes in the cloakroom before going off to our classes. We all had our own lockers in the cloakroom. In the evening, we put our outdoor shoes on again before going home. Getting the cane was not an unusual event, but at the grammar school we got a variation to the norm, and each master had his own form of punishment. With one master at the school, Mr Fred Peart – Ponty Peart we called him – when we did something wrong, he would make us remove a slipper, say "Bend over", and then proceed to whack us on the backside with it. This was the same Fred Peart who after the War took up politics, becoming the Agriculture Minister in Harold Wilson's Labour government, and then – as Baron Peart – Shadow Leader of the House of Lords.

TRAVEL AND TRANSPORTATION

Few people could afford cars, so did not look upon them as a necessary acquisition as people do today. Public transport was the primary method of travelling, whether to visit friends or relatives, to go shopping in Sunderland, or even to go on holiday. Ryhope boasted two railway stations: Ryhope East, which served the route to Seaham and the south, and Ryhope West, which was one of the stations on the line going west to Durham city and the terminus at Old Elvet. This West station was the one used by the miners, their families and the colliery band with its ornate union banner when they went for their annual day out to Durham for the Miner's Gala in July. We had an LNER stationmaster, who lived with his family in a company house beside the East station. But since the stations were only about 200 yards apart, he was in charge of both. The family name was Peacock, and the youngest son, Donald, was with me throughout my school life in Ryhope.

There were a number of bus companies running services to and from Sunderland. The two main companies were the "Blue" bus, namely the Sunderland District Omnibus Company, and the "Red" bus of the Northern Bus Company. Other operators ran services too, such as the Triumph Bus Company, to which I shall refer later, and the Underwood Bus Company, which ceased operating in the mid-1930s.

Within the borough of Sunderland itself, a comprehensive tram system was administered by the Corporation. The most northerly point in this system was the Roker/Seaburn terminal, with Grangetown the southernmost. Many branches of this efficient form of transport spread to other parts of the town, west and east. It was a cheap, regular and dependable method of travel. Many people would even walk the mile-and-a-half from Ryhope to Grangetown to use it. It was also by far the best way of clearing the football crowds from Roker Park on Saturdays (which could number 50,000 or more). The speed and efficiency of this has never been bettered.

In those days, travelling by train was much cheaper than by road. If my memory serves me right, it cost two pence ha'penny for a return ticket from Ryhope to Sunderland by bus, but only three ha'pence by train. When they went shopping to Sunderland on a Saturday, my parents did the same as many others, walking the half mile to the railway station to save the half or one penny difference in the fare. When wages were not so high, it was always essential to economise wherever possible. Every penny had to count.

Travelling on holiday, whether for a day out or on an annual vacation, was also usually by train – though not many people could afford to take a family away because it was an accepted fact that an employee's annual entitlement of a week's holiday had to be taken without pay. Foreign holidays for the working man were out of the question altogether. When you are earning only two or three pounds a week and have a family to raise, such luxuries as holidays away are unthinkable. It must be also remembered that it was in 1936 that the Jarrow Marchers descended on London, demonstrating against the mass unemployment of the time.

I was fortunate in my pre-war youth because I spent much of my summer holidays at the home of my Aunt Sally in Edlington near Doncaster. As mentioned above, she was my father's sister, a widow with one son – Stanley. My father was in a better position than most to afford such holidays because he was in regular, safe employment. However, we still had to economise, so he would wait for the cheap day excursions by the LNER to be announced, then he would buy a cheap day-return for me and himself to Doncaster. He would escort me to my Aunt's, then return home himself. A few weeks later, he would return to take me home again using the same procedure. Two day-returns were cheaper than one ordinary return fare. In most years, my father also went to Aunt Sally's for a week in September to enjoy the racing – the main attraction being the St Leger, for he had always been a keen racing fan.

My first visit to London was in 1937, along with my father and Uncle Jim Carter. He was not really a relation of ours, but a very good friend of my parents from their early days in Sunderland, and whom I had known all my life. He was a lorry driver who delivered goods around County Durham and Tyneside for a Sunderland-based firm called Pearman and Corder, and he often called at our house on his rounds. His son had moved to London with his wife, and we were going to stay with them.

I was already at my Aunt Sally's in Edlington at the time of our trip, so Aunt Sally saw me onto the train at Doncaster, while Dad and Uncle Jim travelled from Sunderland to meet me at King's Cross station. We were all on cheap day-returns. They told me to report to the police box at King's Cross, say I was waiting for my father, and wait there until he arrived. I was sitting in the police box with my case when a policeman came in, looked at me and said: "Is he for Barnardo's?"

My father and Uncle Jim arrived on time as planned. As we walked towards the underground station to travel on to our ultimate destination in Hammersmith, someone approached us to ask if he could have their return tickets. He wanted to go back north but could not even afford the cheaper fare. After all, the day-return tickets we had were of no further use after that day.

What a time I had in the city. I saw and did things my school friends could not imagine. I visited places most of them had only ever heard about or seen at the cinema. I went to the Tower of London to see the Crown Jewels, I saw Buckingham Palace, and best of all I went to the Kensington Science Museum. What a wonder it was for a young boy to play with all the gadgets there, operating them with the turn of a handle or by pressing a button. I talked about the museum for years afterwards. Almost every morning, just after breakfast, I went on my own to Ravenscourt Park and rode for an hour on the motor boats on the lake. It was a wonderful experience. I saw films in the cinemas that would take months to reach Ryhope, and boasted about it to my pals afterwards. The film I most remembered was The Plainsman in which Gary Cooper took the part of Wild Bill Hickock. Even today when it is shown as an "oldie" on television, I think of my first holiday in London. Today, it would be almost unthinkable for a boy to go on his own to London at the age of eleven, let alone going out on his own to ride the boats. How times have changed.

OUTBREAK OF THE SECOND WORLD WAR

On 1 September 1939 I was still on my summer holidays, unlike my pals at the secondary modern, who started the autumn term earlier than we did. It came over the radio that Germany had invaded Poland that day. It was a Friday, I recall. I still remember meeting my pals coming out of school and telling them that war had started. Britain's declaration of war against Germany was made on Sunday 3 September by the Prime Minister, Neville Chamberlain.

The day on which war was declared seemed little different from any other. But when I left the house shortly after the declaration, I did what everyone else did that day: I took my gas mask with me. These had been issued to everyone prior to the commencement of hostilities. The ordinary mask issued to most people was in a cardboard box. You placed a length of string through it so it could be carried over your shoulder, and it was considered an essential item to wear when leaving home. It wasn't long before the novelty wore off and the mask was left at home to be carried only when considered necessary.

The other immediate indication of hostilities was the blackout. Every building had to have something to cover the windows after dark so that no light might be seen by enemy aircraft. Not even a chink was permitted. Air raid wardens would traverse the streets and warn any erring householder or shopkeeper to put out their lights. Air raid wardens were civilian volunteers who were issued with steel helmets and armbands with the letters ARP displayed. But they still performed their day jobs.

A goodly number of households and assorted establishments had their windows covered with tape or a kind of clear varnish to minimise any shattering if there was a bomb blast.

Many people were given Anderson shelters to place in their gardens. Our house was no exception. My father dug a large hole in the garden, the corrugated sections of the shelter were placed in the hole, and then they were covered with much of the soil that had been removed to make the hole. A small entrance was left for the family to enter when an air raid occurred. My parents made the inside of the shelter reasonably comfortable, with seating, extra clothing and blankets ready in case we had to stay there for longer periods of time. Whenever the sirens sounded we would enter the shelter and stay until the all clear was given. As with the gas masks however, we became accustomed to the raids. So we didn't use the shelter every time the warnings were given, but only if we felt danger was near – such as if we heard the approach of an enemy plane, or if bombs were heard dropping nearby. There were quite a number of brick-built shelters erected in Ryhope, primarily to accommodate those people who did not have the garden for an Anderson shelter. These brick shelters were likely to be placed on spare land at the end of a street. At the sound of the sirens, families would leave their homes and proceed to these communal shelters. Some larger shelters were also built on school grounds for the pupils. We had about three of them in the fields of the grammar school.

It was not uncommon to hear fighter planes engaging the enemy, or to see their vapour trails in the sky. There were many nights when a raid was on, and we would hear the shrapnel from the anti-aircraft guns falling onto the roof of the house. We would often pick up pieces of metal in the streets the day after a raid. I remember being rudely awakened early one morning by the sound of machine gun fire. I watched through my bedroom window as a fighter plane chased a runaway barrage balloon until it finally succeeded in setting it on fire, at which the balloon gradually fell to earth.

At the beginning of the war, food was not rationed. It took a while for the government to bring in the appropriate legislation and issue ration books to us all. Until rationing began, there was a period when certain necessary items were in short supply, such as sugar or butter, and we would have to go looking for shops where we thought stocks might be available. This was during the period of the so-called phoney war, when little was happening in France. The headlines in the newspapers were mostly about minor skirmishes over there, raids by the RAF on targets such as shipping in the Kiel Canal, or small air raids in this country.

Changes were taking place around us that were accepted as normal, war-time events. An anti-aircraft battery was built with a camp between Ryhope and Sunderland. Buildings were taken over to serve as headquarters for the air-raid wardens, and of course the number of uniformed personnel you saw on the street increased. An emergency hospital was erected on a green field site near to the mental hospital in Ryhope, to prepare for the anticipated wounded servicemen. Many men began vanishing from the shops and businesses as their call-up notices were served or they volunteered to join the fight. My brother-in-law Jack Rourke (the husband of my sister Ivy) worked in the grocery department of the Co-op, and he was one of those called up. He left to join the R.A.F. and was initially stationed at Stranraer.

At the beginning of the war, all the schools were closed. Mine remained closed for a month or two before we started going back for lessons – initially for only half a day each week. I cannot remember exactly why this happened, but it may have been to allow time for the brick air raid shelters to be built on the fields just beyond the school boundary, to accommodate all the pupils in the event of a raid. We boys looked forward to the breaks in lessons when the sirens sounded, because we did not just sit inside the shelters waiting for the all-clear, or continue with our lessons. Instead, the teachers organised games, sing-songs or mini-concerts to keep us occupied until the all-clear sounded.

BOYHOOD ACTIVITIES
AND ORGANISATIONS

In my friendships with other youngsters nearby, we played many forms of games, many of them all but forgotten by children today. We gave them such names as mount-a-kitty, knocky nine-doors, and so on. Some games were played in specific seasons, yet no one knew the date when they started. You just started playing them without prompting. We had games that involved cigarette cards, marbles, spinning tops with whips, hoop bowling or hide-and-seek.

We had to play these games, as there was nothing else. The radio was mainly for adults, especially in the evenings after six o'clock when children's hour ceased. Apart from Radio Luxembourg there were no commercial stations. Broadcasting had only started 10-15 years before, so it was still in its infancy. Television was a thing of the future. Indoor games such as monopoly or snakes and ladders were available for rainy days or evenings. But outdoor activities were preferred to all others. We even played football and other games around the feeble light of the gas lamps in the streets.

There was one person of whom we young boys were always wary, and that was the village bobby, PC Stubbs. In those days, Ryhope had its own police station with a sergeant in charge. He lived in the police house attached to the station, and there was a regular shift system operating, with bobbies patrolling the streets day and night.

PC Stubbs lived in a house near where our gang played, so it wasn't difficult for him to keep an eye on us. Unlike today, the bobby was someone to fear if you did anything wrong. One day we were playing in a field beside his house when there was snow on the ground. Then someone saw him coming, and with one shout we were off. Young Vince Hudson lost a shoe running in the snow, but did he stop to retrieve it? Did he heck!

He just kept running with the rest of us, such was the power of the bobby.

One of the week's highlights was the Saturday afternoon matinee at the Grand (an odd name for what some people would have called a fleapit). The front stalls were plain wooden benches with back rests. The rear stalls were also wooden, but were individual, tip-up seats. The balcony was the only area in the cinema with some form of upholstery on the seating. We kids would queue up on a Saturday afternoon at the side entrance (normally used for the front stalls; it was never the front door for us on matinee days). Mr Money would then usher us in, at a cost of 1d. Sometimes he filled the seats from the front row and worked backwards, while at other times he filled them from the back to the front. So it was no good trying to get a good position in the queue. You just didn't know where he would start that week. No one liked to sit in the front row because it meant looking almost vertically at the screen.

The shows always consisted of shorts and comedies, then the afternoon finished off with an adventure serial. This serial would have five or six episodes in all. The hero was always engaged in some dangerous adventure, and at the end of each episode he would be in a difficult situation that left us guessing how he might escape. The ending might have a car going over a cliff, or an aeroplane in which our hero was sent crashing to the ground. The following week we waited eagerly to find out what had happened – only to learn that he had jumped out of the car or the plane just before the crash. We were relieved to see he lived again to save the maiden in distress.

My parents were keen whist players. Whist drives were quite popular in general, and every Saturday evening there was a whist drive at the church institute to which my parents went. When I was younger they took me along so as to know where I was whilst they played. In any case, there were other children there and we kept ourselves occupied. I actually enjoyed it because we would be given packets of sweets or potato crisps (with a small, separate packet of salt inside).

Friday nights offered another night out at the pictures, this time in the theatre at the mental hospital. The entertainment was actually provided for the patients. But I was entitled to go too, since my father worked at the hospital and children of employees were allowed to attend all their shows. The films were of the silent variety, but we would sit enthralled while Mr Tommy Young, one of the male nurses, provided the piano accompaniment in the usual silent movie style. And every fourth Friday there was a concert party instead of movies. There were singers, conjurors, and so on, and the hospital staff provided the orchestra – there were a few good instrumentalists among them.

The final example of picture entertainment that I recall was provided by the Salvation Army. They had their citadel on Burdon Road. It was a newish building, and they regularly held magic lantern shows there, which I believe cost ½d per showing. The performance consisted of a picture projected on to a screen, while a member of the Army would recite a story as the pictures were changed. It wasn't exactly thrilling, but to us pre-war kids it was another means of entertainment.

We boys often spent our holidays down at Ryhope beach. On fine days we would go there to paddle, search the rock pools for crabs and sea creatures, build fires with drift wood and cook whelks which we had gathered. We just had a great time altogether, and it was a wonderful place for adventure. Living near to the sea, I could not understand my relations near Doncaster who regarded their annual trips to Cleethorpes as wonderful and something to talk about all year. Later in my working life I had to go to Immingham on business. So I felt I had to call in to see nearby Cleethorpes to see just what my relations had enthused over. I went and thought: Urgh! Perhaps it had been allowed to run down after the war. Or perhaps it had always been like that, and I was just more fortunate than them, but did not appreciate what I had.

The large hall at the hospital that served as its theatre was also the venue for the hospital church. The hospital had its own church choir, choirmaster, organist and all, and it was another instance of employees' children getting involved in the life of the place. When I was 10 or 11 years old my father took me to the home of a Mr Richardson (who was also a male nurse) for an audition for the hospital church choir. I had a good treble voice when I was young, so I passed the test with ease. Every Sunday morning thereafter, I went to sing at the hospital service. The Church of England priest was always in attendance. Every Thursday evening was choir practice. Mr Young – the same who was the pianist for the pictures – was also the organist for the hospital church. Mr Richardson was the choir master. The choir was about ten strong, and occasionally we had the odd male baritone, bass, or tenor from among the members of the hospital staff. As a result of my association with the hospital choir, the quality of my voice became known to the vicar, so sometimes I got an invitation to sing in the St Paul's Church choir when they were shorthanded. The advantage we hospital choir boys had over the church boys was our rate of pay. We received 6d per week, paid on a monthly basis, whereas the St Paul's lot were lucky to earn two shillings a quarter. The highlight of the choirboys' year was at Christmas, when we toured all the wards in the hospital singing carols. Then at the end of the evening we had a really good party with lots to eat, plus paper hats, balloons and so on.

One of the curates who took the hospital services on Sundays was a Mr Mercer. He had a car that had a 'Dicky seat' – that was a seat where the boot is situated in cars today. The lid would pull back to reveal two seats. We boys loved to be given a ride after the service in Mr Mercer's Dicky seat, open to the air and in a position where we could wave to anyone we passed. The station master Mr Peacock had twin boys as well as Donald. They were well noted for their devilment, and I still remember them riding with the curate in his car, sitting in the Dicky, one of them resting his feet on the curate's shoulder while the other twin had his feet on the back of the front passenger seat. Of course, this was in the days long before seat belts were common.

The hospital was virtually a self-sufficient unit. As the upholsterer, my father repaired all the furniture and curtains.

There was also a joiner, a cobbler, an electrician and a tailor, and the hospital even had its own bakery, with a baker called Mr Clarke. A farm provided meat from its pigs and milk and cream from its herd of cows. There was also a market garden to supply vegetables. To top it all, the hospital had its own power station, with coal-fired boilers. If they were able, the patients would help the artisans, the farmer or whoever else required assistance. Apart from being a form of therapy, this also gave the patients a way of being useful in the running of the hospital, and probably stopped them from becoming bored. In addition to the patients, the medical and administrative staff, the farm hands and their families, there were many people dependent upon the hospital for their livelihood. There was also living accommodation for some of the staff and their families, though it was only available on a limited basis.

I had a friend called Tommy Openshaw who had been taught how to play the church bells at St Paul's and who offered to teach me too. We practiced on weekday evenings. The bell room was situated above the entrance to the church, and you reached it by means of a winding staircase through a door at the side. Ropes from each of the six bells came down into the bell ringers' room, close to the wall. Two wooden brackets were fixed to the wall, like two shelves, the one about two feet below the other. Bell ropes were threaded through holes drilled into these brackets. The ropes below the lower bracket were secured so that if you pulled the rope towards you, it rang the bell. You could play a certain peal or tune by pulling the ropes in particular sequences. Before I became a fully-fledged bell ringer, however, the war started. Church bells were stopped during the war – they were to be used only as a signal that the Germans were invading England.

There was one other activity that involved the church, though only on an occasional basis – pumping up the large organ. One of my friends, Billy Fishwick, played the piano and organ very well, so there were times when he was asked to play the church organ at weddings. But the organ was not electrically operated and the bellows had to be pumped by hand. So now and then he asked me to help out, and I would get a shilling or two out of his fee for my troubles.

CUBS AND SCOUTS

Like many of my friends, I was a member of the scout movement – first in the cubs, then from 1937 in the scouts proper, as a member of the St Paul's Church scout troop. The cub mistress was Ruth Hunt, the scout master Eric Kennedy. They married when I was in the scouts, so we formed a guard of honour when they left the church on their wedding day.

My first camp away from home was with the cubs to a field on the edge of some woods near the town of Prudhoe, west of Newcastle. Although it lies only some twenty miles from Ryhope, I can still remember that the dialect of the area was quite different from our own on Wearside. This was the first time I can remember hearing the Northumbrian burr. Some parents came to visit us. Mine travelled with Alan Yeaman's parents, who as I mentioned earlier were one of the few families to own a car. Getting to Prudhoe was much easier with private transport, since there was no direct bus or train. Many camps away followed over the years and all were most enjoyable. One particular camping spot was at Sharpley, a camping ground for all the scout troops in the Sunderland area (after the War began, travelling to camps that weren't close to home was discouraged). Sharpley lay between Houghton-le-Spring and Seaham, only about three miles from Ryhope. We had a trek cart (a must for all good scout troops) that we used to push up Burdon Road loaded with gear, though a lot of the heavy equipment, such as tents, was kept permanently on the site, for each troop had its own storage area there. It was on one of these short trips to Sharpley at the beginning of the war that there was an amusing interlude. The Home Guard were on exercises in the neighbourhood. One of our members – Bobby Henderson – strayed to the edge of the woods when he heard a voice boom out at him: "Halt! Who goes there?" Bobby got a shock, had no idea where the voice had come from, and could only shout back: "Me!" He was ribbed about this for years after.

When war was declared, the authorities said that everyone should become economy-minded, doing such things as recycling newspapers. This was supposed to help free up transport for essential items for the war effort. We boy scouts did our bit, touring the streets of Ryhope with our trek cart, calling at houses to collect unwanted magazines and newspapers, and then taking them back to our scout hut where they were collected and delivered to the appropriate depot.

In 1940, when the Germans overran France and our troops were evacuated via Dunkirk, there were many wounded servicemen. Many trains bearing the mark of the Red Cross started bringing injured men to the emergency hospital in Ryhope. We scouts were on hand to help, and we spent time going round the wards, running messages or pushing trolleys loaded with items from a local shop to help cater for the servicemen's needs. There were many French troops there, too, and I remember going into the wards in my Boy Scout uniform and practising my French with servicemen there. Soldiers in hospital who were able to go out – in other words, those who had recovered sufficiently to be able to walk into Ryhope – were issued with "hospital blues". These clothes were the same as their battle dress, but blue in colour, quite different from the normal khaki of a military uniform. These wounded men were a common sight in Ryhope village during the war.

There was one other function that the St Paul's scout troop performed at the start of the War. No one had any experience of air raids, so the vicar arranged with the police for a member of the scout troop to sit in the police station while he conducted his Sunday service. The police got advance notice of any air raid warning. If such a warning was about to be made, the police would tell the scout on duty, who then had to run to the church, 200 yards away, to alert the congregation. But after a few months, this duty was phased out because there never were any air raids during a Sunday church service.

ELOCUTION LESSONS

Bob's recitation at a Burn's supper as reported in the Sunderland Echo, 1936

My first appearance on stage in front of a large audience was in about 1931, when I took part in a concert organised in the Victoria Hall in Sunderland by the local Anglican community. I cannot recollect what it was about, but I do remember sitting on someone's knee and having to say the words: "I am so tired". The Victoria Hall no longer exists, as it was destroyed in a bombing raid during the Second World War.

The real foundations of my stage life were laid some four or five years later, thanks to two people I mentioned earlier who had a considerable impact on my later life: Miss Eales, my elocution teacher, and Mr John Phillips, my piano teacher. Many houses had pianos before the war, and we were no exception. Shortly after we moved to Gray Terrace, I started to learn the piano under Mr Phillips. By a strange coincidence, I much later learnt that my wife Bess had also studied the piano with him. A few months after starting the piano, my parents informed me that I was going to have elocution lessons with Miss Eales. I believe my parents didn't want me to grow up with a distinct Wearside dialect, and thought that taking the edge off it would improve my chances of a good start in life.

Music lessons are self-explanatory, but to be honest, I did not even know what elocution was at the time. Like my piano teacher, Miss Eales came to our house to give me a lesson once a week. We would go into the front room for me to do my exercises in enunciation. I had to practice speaking clearly and correctly, going through the vowels and speaking them in the appropriate manner. I often did this by learning tongue-twisters, or sentences where the vowels were prominent. One example I remember was: "Old oily Olly oils old oily autos". Miss Eales also gave me verse and poetry to memorise, and the following week I was expected to recite it all, giving emphasis with both vocal and physical expression so as to increase the listener's understanding and pleasure. Over time, I graduated to longer verse and monologues, once again trying to deliver them with expression and, where necessary, a hint of dialect. The first monologue I learned was one that was often broadcast by Stanley Holloway: "Albert and the Lion", most of which I can remember to this day.

At least once each year, Miss Eales got her pupils together to put on a show for the parents, either by giving their party pieces or performing a group play. It also became a regular practice for my parents to ask me to give a recitation whenever they took me out with them to visit friends. But I would sometimes become bored with all this and would refuse to go visiting with them.

Mr Phillips also happened to be the organist at St John's Church in Seaham, and he invited the odd pupil of his to the church to see if they would like to try the organ. I went a few times but never got the hang of it. Mr Phillips was also in demand as a pianist and singer at functions such as Burn's night suppers or at Masonics. He heard of my recitation skills and asked my parents if he could take me to these affairs, and so began my life as a performer. It would be reported in the Sunderland Echo that there was a concert at such-and-such a place, with entertainment provided by Mr Phillips "with recitations by Master R Walton".

I also performed in school plays (where my English teacher Mr Deans put in one of my school reports "Acts well in drama"). The Second World War curtailed my appearances, but by then I was in any case at the local Grammar school, studying for my School Certificate, and such work had to take precedence over any sorties into the world of entertainment. I did, however, take part in concerts organised by the school to raise funds for the war effort.

SERVICE LIFE

New recruits at HMS Royal Arthur, 1945.
Bob in the third row, third from right

Children of my generation normally left school at fourteen to start earning a living. But we at grammar school were expected to continue our education until at least sixteen when we sat the Oxford School Certificate. Its broader, deeper range of subject matter gave us a considerable advantage over many others of our generation. But the war had an interrupting influence on all our lives. So while I took my School Certificate examination and obtained good results – no failures, mainly credits and distinctions – I decided to leave and commence work, knowing full well that I would be called up for the armed forces anyway. I could have stayed on for my highers, but would still have had to do my time in the forces. University would have had to wait.

There was practically no chance of getting an uninterrupted path to a degree like there is today, and it would have taken me five or six years, even without the war. In any case, after demob it took me more than double that time to acquire professional status and membership of the Royal Institute of Chemistry.

In my short pre-service life, I was given a few months' training in the handling and analysis of explosives at Leys School in Cambridge. On completion of that training I was despatched to a chemical laboratory in Irvine in Ayrshire in Scotland, working for the Ministry of Supply, analysing explosives and their constituents. The primary explosive was TNT, though contrary to the perceived notion of it, it wasn't too dangerous unless in some form of sealed container. My colleagues and I often put a light to bits of TNT in a fume cupboard and watched the flames and great clouds of gas that were formed.

I was working up in Scotland when I received word that I had to attend a medical examination for my call-up. This took place in Glasgow, and I was passed "A1". The one worry for many young men like myself was that we could be assigned to be Bevin Boys, named after Ernest Bevin, the Minister of Labour. Because of the vital importance of coal to the war effort and the shortage of coalminers, Bevin had decreed that a percentage of those called up to serve in the armed forces should instead go to work in the coalmines. My call-up papers duly came and luckily my name did not come out of the hat as a Bevin Boy. It was the Navy for me, and I had to report to HMS Royal Arthur in early 1945. This was actually the Butlins holiday camp at Skegness, which had been commandeered at the start of the war and was now a training base for all naval entrants. There we were given further medical examinations, given naval uniforms, a kit bag, and all our clothing from top to toe. We were also issued with a hammock and a mattress. It was the custom in the Navy to issue winter and summer dress on joining. Normally we sailors wore the round cap which perched on the head, which was coloured blue, as was the woollen jumper that we wore under our tunic. In summer, however, the woollen jumper was replaced with a white cotton shirt edged with blue tape. The hat was also white for summer dress. The Navy was different from the other services in that after you received your first issue of clothing, hammock, mattress, etc., you were expected to buy their replacements when they became worn. For this, you received 6d per day extra with your pay. This is why in ports where there were large naval establishments there were many naval tailors. You could not get stirred in Queen Street in Portsmouth for naval tailors.

One firm called "Bernards" seemed to be the largest, and they had many branches throughout the country. If he wished, a sailor could buy his kit at the "Pusser's" store, this being the Navy's own store, which sold gear more cheaply. But the better quality of materials at the private tailors and the fact that they made to measure meant that this supplier was preferred, and offered a much better fit. The "Pusser's" store was OK for such things as shoe brushes or hammocks, but not for the fashion-conscious young sailor who could afford to buy his uniform privately.

It was obligatory that every item of clothing a sailor possessed was stamped with his name – literally everything, from boots to hat. The Navy issued us with a wooden stamp bearing our name. Then, using marking ink, we stamped our name on a section of clothing not visible from the outside. The only exception was our boots. For these, you had to get a metal stamp that cut into the leather. There was one chap slightly older than most of us who had a distinct problem, for his surname was very long: I still remember it: Stack-Poole-Riding, and that was without his initials. He had to get more than one stamp to do the job. Sailors were always reluctant to spend their clothing allowance unnecessarily, though there was an alternative, because the Admiralty would now and then have a sale of very cheap second clothing. It was called a "DC sale", which stood for "Dead Man's Clothing". It may have been someone who had been killed or who had died unexpectedly. The proceeds – so we were told – went to the relatives of the deceased. In true naval fashion, the items were marked with indelible ink DC, but you still had to put your own name on them. I still have a collar in my kitbag with the DC stamp on it.

We were housed in chalets that the holiday makers used in the days when HMS Royal Arthur was a Butlins holiday camp. Of course, all the facilities for feeding hungry men were there, with large dining halls and all the necessary kitchen cooking equipment along with dishwashing machines. There was plenty of open space for square bashing, sports halls and grounds for recreation, and even a large boating lake where we learned all about longboats and how to row them. The only thing was that the boats were fastened to the shore with long chains, and the oars had holes in them. This meant that we could learn the rudiments of rowing, but were not able to stray from the bank. I often told this story of the boats to my colleagues at I.C.I. They thought I was joking until one day I went to work and saw on the notice board a cutting from a national newspaper recalling these facts of early naval training in the war. Someone had read it and thought it worth displaying, so wrote "Bob's Boat" on top. After this, they believed everything I told them. At HMS Royal Arthur, we were taught the basics of seamanship and service life, from tying knots to rifle shooting on the ranges. We had to realise that there was strict discipline in service life – more than we had been led to believe before joining up.

While we were stationed at Royal Arthur we were assessed by Wrens whose task was to find out what job we might be suitable to do during our service in the Navy. After answering certain questions and having discussions with my assessor, she suggested that I should train as a naval photographer. I was quite happy with this because I did not fancy being a stoker, steward or suchlike. Going to the Royal Naval School of Photography, however, had to wait until I had completed all my basic training.

It was at Royal Arthur that I became acquainted with the peculiar aspects of life in the Navy. For example, we had to use naval terms for many things. We had to refer to Royal Arthur as the "ship", and when going out for the night we were "going ashore", and had to wait for the "Liberty Boat" – we could not just casually walk out to go into town. At designated times we were told that the liberty boats were due to leave and ratings had to assemble to go ashore. Each group representing a boat would march out together and then disperse outside. After a certain time, say at 6pm, they would pipe "Free Gangway" over the tannoy system. This meant that individuals could walk ashore when they wished. The ground was always the "deck", walls the "bulkhead", toilets the "heads", the parade ground the "quarter deck", and so forth. And when replying to an order or request, you always answered: "Aye aye, Sir."

Another thing specific to the Navy, not found in the other services, was how they gave you your pay. The men formed ranks in front of the paymaster. Then, when your name was called, you stepped forward, shouted out your service number (in my case L/MX742974, the L denoting my port division of Lee-on-Solent, MX for miscellaneous trade), you saluted, swiftly removed your hat and placed it on the table. Your money was then put on top of your hat, which you picked up along with your money before smartly returning to your position in the ranks. We were paid the princely sum of 2 shillings per day, handed out once every two weeks to the nearest 10 shillings down. This meant that for the first fortnight you got £1 (20 shillings); at the next payday you would be entitled to 36 shillings, but only received 30 shillings. In other words, they always owed you.

Another peculiarity was the matter of growing a beard. The Navy was the only section of the armed forces that permitted men to grow a beard. However, if you were clean shaven and wished to grow "a set", you had to make a formal request, and then permission would be granted. The one condition, if I recall correctly, was that you had to stay aboard ship until the beard was of a reasonable size and looked respectable. You then had to have your photograph taken again and the picture stuck into your pay book. When this was done, permission was given to venture ashore.

The next step in basic training came after about a month at Skegness. I was transferred to HMS Iron Duke at Malvern in

Worcester, certainly nowhere near the sea. It must be remembered that all naval establishments were given the prefix HMS, and everything there was geared to life on board ship. Woe betide anyone who didn't use the naval terminology mentioned above. We did more seamanship at Iron Duke, with rifle and bayonet training and unarmed combat. We were also given lectures on what we could not do as members of the Royal Navy, at home or abroad.

It was about this time that I became acquainted with the two main perks of Navy personnel compared to the other services: tickler and rum. Tickler was duty-free naval tobacco that you were allowed to buy once each month. When this ration was due, you were given the choice of having:

1. One pound of leaf tobacco, or
2. one pound of pipe tobacco, or
3. one pound of cigarette tobacco, or
4. four hundred Navy-made cigarettes.

The cost of any one of the above was the ridiculous sum of four shillings. Not many ratings bought the leaf tobacco, though some of the older salts preferred it. These men would cut out the stalks on the tobacco leaves, sprinkle some of their rum ration on the leaves, then finally roll the leaves in cloth to form plugs that were made tight by rolling string around them, pulling it tight and then tying it off. These plugs of tobacco would be left for a week or two, then unrolled to reveal a rum-soaked plug ready for cutting up for their pipe or for chewing.

The second perk, of course, was the daily tot of rum. Every day approaching mid-day, the call would come over the tannoy: "Leading hands of messes for rum". The representative of the mess would then pick up the special container provided in every mess and proceed to the galley. There, an officer, a petty officer and other ratings acting as clerks were waiting with ledgers to mark off when the rum was issued to the appropriate mess. The rum was served from a large wooden barrel on the side of which were the words "The King God Bless Him" in brass lettering. The leading hand of a mess would step forward and shout out the number of his mess. The clerk then called out the number of ratings eligible, and the appropriate amount of rum would be measured and poured into the container. The leading hand then took it back to the mess. At noon, the ratings came in from their labours and the leading hand – also called the "bubbly bosun" – poured out their ration into each man's cup using a measure (about 1/8th of a pint). Then, with a quick flick of the wrist, the man receiving it would pour back a small amount into the large container. This was the bubbly bosun's reward for going to the galley for the rum. It was a custom in the Navy to reward anyone who did you a favour with what we termed "sippers", namely a small amount of your rum ration. Since the bubbly bosun did you a favour by going for the rum, he was entitled to this form of payment. For a larger favour, a man would be rewarded with "gulpers", in other words a really good swallow of rum. Sadly today, there is no more rum ration given to naval ratings, for the practice was halted in 1970. I wonder how friends are repaid in the Navy today for any favours if there isn't any rum?

There were times when we received extra rations of rum. These were special occasions such as the King's birthday. Then the order would be given: "Splice the mainbrace", and double rations were issued. However, if people were teetotal and didn't want their grog, then they could opt to have an extra 3d per day to their pay. Very few men did this. After all, you could use the tot to get others to do you many a good turn, so it was worth much more than 3d a day.

I remember HMS Iron Duke for two particular reasons. It was there that I saw my first banana in six years. Someone had been "ashore", a relation of his had given him a banana, and he brought it back to show us. This was the only time I've ever known grown men queuing in a crowded room to see a fruit. Secondly, it was here that I remember seeing a man actually desert. We were playing football on a field attached to the base when this chap playing on the wing ran straight down past the goalkeeper and off the field. The petty officer in charge was astounded – he just couldn't believe it. The rating was found a week or two later at his home in Birmingham, and brought back. I don't know what happened to him.

There were many American service men's camps in England, and quite a few in the Midlands near to us. We often met these men in and around Malvern. One Sunday they provided us ratings with an unexpectedly entertaining afternoon and evening. Their units were having a big band competition. It was supposed to be a grand, open-air event, but the weather wasn't too kind that day, so arrangements were hastily made to hold it in our base hall. All of us were invited to this musical extravaganza, and we had a great time listening to all those top-class players.

The war was coming to an end, and when Germany surrendered there were celebrations and victory parades throughout the country. Malvern wasn't too far from Birmingham, and word came that we sailors were needed to participate in the victory parade in the city, along with representatives of the other services. So we travelled to Birmingham and took our place in a ceremonial march-past in front of the Lord Mayor and senior members of the armed forces. I took part in another parade not long after, when Japan capitulated. By this time I had been transferred to Lee-on-Solent, and this march-past took place in Portsmouth.

TRANSFERRED TO
THE FLEET AIR ARM

I was transferred from HMS Iron Duke to my port division, the headquarters of the Fleet Air Arm, HMS Daedalus in Lee-on-Solent. Photographers were classed as air crew and thus members of the Fleet Air Arm. Lee-on-Solent was an airfield near Gosport. Leaving Iron Duke on the same draft with me were a number of other ratings going to join their port divisions at Portsmouth, Gosport and elsewhere. We were transported across London from St Pancras to Waterloo station to catch our trains heading south. While we were travelling across town in the back of an open lorry, we stopped at some traffic lights. Alongside us, a lorry laden with apples and other fruit pulled up, so one of the lads leaned over and took some of it to pass around before we and the fruit lorry moved away when the lights changed to green.

Many of the ratings in Lee-on-Solent were en route to new postings, but they were not allowed to remain idle. They were allocated jobs such as clerks, messengers, cleaners and so on. One job I was given whilst awaiting transfer was cleaning and tidying up the offices in the HQ. I had to dust the officers' desks, empty their ashtrays, etc. There were five or six of us doing this, and we had a couple of wide boys, always on the make. They would save all the large cigarette ends from the ashtrays – of which there were plenty because of the cheap tobacco – and then they would strip off the paper on the cigarette ends, cut off the burnt ends of tobacco, break up the rest, put it in Tickler tins (i.e. Navy tobacco tins) and sell it to any civilian employee on the base who was willing to buy it, thinking it was genuine tickler tobacco.

It was still the time of compulsory church parades, so every Sunday morning we had to gather for church. We would line up on the quarterdeck (i.e. the parade ground), then the chief petty officer would call out "Church of England on the right, Roman

Catholics on the left, Methodists, Wesleyans, atheists in the centre". Thus assembled, we marched off to our various places of worship.

There was one chap in our mess with whom I was quite friendly. He was black, and had the flash "Barbados" on the shoulder of his jacket, indicating where he came from. The only problem was, as the only black person in Lee-on-Solent, poor Vic could never escape parades or do anything untoward because he stood out and was easily recognised. I felt sorry for him at times.

At Lee-on-Solent I had to wait a few weeks before the next course at the school of photography began. It was now late June or early July 1945. I put in a request for my first leave somewhat earlier than normal because I wished to attend my sister Doreen's wedding. My request was granted, and I set off home for the first time in the uniform of a sailor. The train was not long out of Kings Cross station when a member of the WAAF came along the aisle. She tried to open the connecting door to the next carriage, but failed, whereupon she turned to me and asked "Excuse me, sailor, can you help me?". There I was, still wet behind the ears, and being called "sailor" – I felt like Popeye getting his spinach, so I boldly stood up and displayed whatever strength I had to help the young lady from the RAF gain access to the next carriage.

On returning from leave to Lee I was allocated another job: guarding the officers' gate. This entailed four hours on, four hours off, then a twenty-four hour break. Standing in the guard box was tedious at times, and we had to salute every officer that passed through the gate. This meant bringing the rifle down from your shoulder and presenting arms. Given the number of officers coming through, it could be quite tiring. I recall one incident quite clearly while I was on guard duty. An officer from the Women's Royal Naval Service (the "Wrens") came through the gate, and I brought my rifle down to the "at ease" position. But she immediately gave me a return salute; this was normal practice for male officers, but we did not present arms for Wren officers because at that time they did not hold the King's Commission, and so were not entitled to a salute. This was why I placed my rifle at ease. When I dropped to that position and spread my feet to easy, she must have thought I was saluting her.

Lee was just across the water from Portsmouth, and we often got transport to Gosport where we could board the Pompey ferry to take us across to the ferry landing at the Portsmouth harbour station. It was here that I saw the Pompey Mudlarks for the first time. These were young boys who stood in the thick mud under the station landing area, from where they would shout up to the people walking above, hoping that they would throw coins down to them. The boys would then dive into the harbour mud and retrieve the coins. One can imagine the state of them after diving into the mud.

In the summer months we often went to Pompey when we had shore leave. We got off the Gosport ferry, then walked from the harbour station to Southsea, which was a nearby holiday resort. Here we would see the shows, visit the fairground, and see some of the top dance bands who performed there, such as the Squadronaires. If we had weekend passes, we could stay in the servicemen's hostels overnight for a small sum. These were just beds set up in rooms and corridors, and you had to get your meals elsewhere. It was always wise to watch your belongings and keep them safe overnight. Some men even put their boots under the legs of the bedposts for safety, meaning no one could steal them without first lifting up the bed – and thus waking its occupant.

Budding photographers at the Royal Naval School of Photography in Felpham, near Bognor Regis in 1945, prior to weeding out after the entrance exams. Bob in the second bottom row, third from the left.

...signed on the back by everyone

OFF TO THE ROYAL NAVAL SCHOOL OF PHOTOGRAPHY

A few weeks after coming off my first leave I was despatched to Felpham near Bognor Regis, to the Royal Naval School of Photography. It was situated on a private housing estate. Six houses had been commandeered to provide living, office, training, and recreational facilities for the naval personnel. This estate was right next to the sea, but as was the custom during the war, you could not access the shore itself because of all the barbed wire on the foreshore.

Thus I began some six months of intensive training in the art of photography. First we did three months of ground work, learning the rudiments of all aspects of photography. We took pictures with a range of cameras and processed the films. We had to get to know all the different types of camera – how they worked, and how to operate them. It was also necessary to do what was called presswork, which meant taking pictures from all angles at very short notice at any distance from the subject, which might even be a moving object. In doing so you had to adjust the camera for depth of focus, set the correct shutter speed, then at the end of it all produce a dozen matching prints, the whole business being done in a specified period of time. A favourite ploy of the petty officer was to jump on a bicycle, pedal towards you then call out: "Front!", "Port!", "Rear!" etc. This meant you had to position yourself quickly, adjust the camera and take a quality picture.

At the end of three months there was an examination: if you didn't pass, then you were off the course, you returned to base and were assigned some other trade in the service. I managed to pass, so I was able to go on to acquire skills in aerial work. Having done all the theory and practice relating to processing and the rest during the first three months, and having become familiar with the range of cameras we were to use, the emphasis was now on flying and on the techniques and skills necessary for the various types of camera and everything else that was required in aerial work.

Photographs taken from the air would be processed, then passed over to assessors who were trained to study and examine them. All the individual photographs that we took of an area were made into a mosaic. We did this by using a razor blade and cutting away the paper on the positive print, leaving the emulsion only. We carefully cut a wavy line through the paper, then eased it away from the emulsion underneath. The idea was that with only the emulsion left we were able to glue the pictures to each other with no lumps at the joins, and all the photographs were then placed in sequence to obtain a large photograph of the area we had shot.

Our first task in aerial work was to get to know the main aircraft used for this type of work, which in our case was the Avro Anson. The Anson had been adapted for aerial reconnaissance duty and had a cradle mounted in the nose of the aircraft beyond the pilot. A large F24 camera rested in this cradle, and it was there that we took our vertical shots. This camera could be adjusted for manual or automatic operation, depending upon the type of work to be done. When using the F24 in position in the cradle, we had to squeeze past the pilot and lie flat on our tummies, looking through the circular window to take our shots.

There was no naval airfield near to Felpham, so we had to go to RAF Ford. The first flight we took was just to get us used to flying. None of us had been in an aircraft before. We put on our flying helmets with built-in radios, slung our parachutes over our shoulders, strapped them on and waddled to the plane. We were shown where we had to sit, where the camera positions were, where we had to go to take shots out of the side of the plane (this was done by lifting up the upper half of the door and hanging out holding the camera), and finally where the fixed camera positions were situated in the aircraft nose. When we were taking photos out of the side windows, we had to have a cord attached to the camera that was then slung round our necks. The petty officer said: "If the camera falls you had better follow it". If we felt we were going to be airsick, we were shown where to go – but then on landing we had to pay the aircraft fitter 2/6d because he was the one who had to clear up the mess.

After the initial flight we were on our own from then on in. We would be given instructions on the ground about the flight, what area we had to cover, and what type of photographs were wanted – whether oblique shots with a handheld camera, or vertical shots with the F24 camera fixed to the floor in the nose of the aircraft, or even perhaps both. This all entailed making a lot of calculations beforehand with regard to the height and speed of the aircraft, the wind drift and so on. Since the photographer studied and calculated everything relating to the mission beforehand, and since he knew the target and the path to be taken for a mosaic picture, it was understood that once we began shooting, it was the photographer who was in charge of the aircraft. The pilot had to fly where the photographer ordered. We had to make sure the pilot flew in the predetermined line for the series of shots as we lay down in the nose of the aircraft, and issued orders such as "A little to port" or "A little to starboard". The pilot was told when the run was complete and could make his turn to commence a new run.

There was one amusing side to this flying, at least by modern day standards, and that was that the Avro Anson did not have electrically operated flaps or landing gear. So when we took off, if there was only you and the pilot, he would say over the intercom: "Wheels, please", which meant we had to turn a handle down to our right and count the turns to ensure the wheels were fully retracted. The same procedure took place on landing: "Wheels down please", then, shortly afterwards, "Flaps, please". Once again, the turns were counted to make sure that the wheels were down, then the flaps lever was pumped a certain number of times to ensure that they were fully down for landing position. I heard of one incident when the photographer got his instructions for the wheels on take-off, but mistakenly operated the flaps instead.

It was only thanks to the pilot's skill that they managed to clear the nearby roofs.

I passed my final exam at the Photography School, and returned to my port division to await assignment. We were given leave before returning to Lee-on-Solent. Being in the Navy meant that you didn't just have to carry a kit bag and small hand luggage everywhere, but also your hammock and mattress. Imagine going on leave and having to carry all this while changing trains! The trains back then were always full and you would be lucky to get a seat at all. So I did what one old sailor told me: I spoke to the guard on the train to get permission to sling my hammock across the width of the guard's van (it was possible to fasten the hammock ropes near the window bars). So I rode in comfort all the way from Kings Cross while others were jostling in the corridors.

Things in the Navy were never swift, so I had to wait two or three months before I got word about my transfer. Six of us newly qualified photographers were called to the drafting Master-at-Arms. He ordered us to go and get tropical kit, inoculations and so on, and gave us passes for fourteen days of foreign draft leave before telling us we were heading for Ukussa in Ceylon. So off I went on my leave, said goodbye to my mum and dad, and returned to Lee-on-Solent. Another month went by. Then we were called again by the Master-at-Arms. This time he said: "Right! You're not going to Ceylon". Then, pointing to me and another chap, he said: "You two are going to West Wales, and the rest of you to Malta". That meant I was headed for HMS Goldcrest in Pembrokeshire, an airfield belonging to Western Command, situated right on the coast near to a village called Dale, to the west of Haverfordwest. Opposite the base were the islands of Skomer and Skokholm.

I thoroughly enjoyed my time there. There were two of us "snaps", plus a petty officer. We were virtually a self-contained unit. The other photographer was a Welshman named Wynford Asaph Williams – "Taffy" – who hailed from the outskirts of Swansea. He was a Welsh speaker who had not spoken English until he was 11 years old, he said. He had even taken English as his foreign language when he sat his School Certificate. Taffy and I were allowed to live in the photographic section, situated on the edge of the airfield about three-quarters of a mile from the rest of the personnel. We would often eat in the main galley because it was near to the NAAFI and also to the cinema, in other words where all activities and entertainment took place. If we were not going anywhere, however, we could eat at home, as it were. Taffy had a pal from his home area working in the food stores. He would ring him up and ask in Welsh: "Has he gone yet?", meaning the petty officer. If his friend said "yes", then Taff and I would go down to the stores and replenish our stocks of grub, for the petty officer would never allow it if he were there. The other source of food nearby was a farm next to the airfield. We had an arrangement with the farmer's wife to buy milk, eggs, and other produce from her. All these dealings allowed us considerable independence in our section, and a greater variety of fresh food.

I was always keen on playing and watching football (especially Sunderland AFC), and at HMS Goldcrest there were plenty of opportunities to play the game. I used to help out in the sports store on board, issuing kit, blowing up the balls etc., and so I became involved in running sports on the base. I would referee matches, looking for talent. It wasn't long before I was invited to become a member of the selection committee for the football team, which played in the West Wales Amateur League. We would ensure that the incoming drafts were checked for potential players, and as a result we were successful in procuring men from the professional ranks, some of whom had played for such teams as Wolves, Swansea, Blackburn and elsewhere before being called up into the forces.

I couldn't hope to compete for a place in the team with such quality players available, but being on the committee was the next best thing, and I got to see all the games, both home and away. If we were playing in matches that meant staying overnight somewhere else, then I got free transport, bed and breakfast and a night out with the boys. I did get the occasional game when we were short of players because of transfers, illness or injury, so naturally I had to be registered with the league. There was also a dodge we played with players' registrations. If a good player was drafted to the ship but we hadn't time to register him, then I would give the match officials a list including my name as a player. I would then tell the new boy that if the referee asked his name, he was to say he was "R. Walton". With the quality of players we had, we cleaned up in the West Wales Amateur League and won the West Wales Amateur Cup as well.

As a result of my association with the football team I met a remarkable man, though I did not realise it at the time. His name was Willie Tebb. He was quite a good footballer (a goalkeeper, in fact). We became good friends, and when his wife joined him, they rented a cottage just outside the base. I would often go there for Sunday lunch, and I spent a lot of time in their company. A few months after we met, an article was printed in a newspaper about the attacks on the German battleship Tirpitz in the Norwegian fiords during the War. Willie figured prominently in it. He was one of the members of a group who had been trained to attack the ship in two-man submarines. These subs were slung under fishing trawlers and entered the fiord under the noses of the enemy.

Sunday lunch at Willie Tebb's. From left to right: Willie Tebb, his wife, Petty Officer North, Bob, Petty Officer Collyer

At the appropriate moment, the subs were released from the trawlers, and headed for the Tirpitz. They made their attack and tried to get away, but Willie's sub was damaged. He and his companion scrambled ashore and headed for the Swedish border. But his companion was injured, could not carry on, and so told Willie to go on, while he would wait for the Germans and get the medical treatment he needed. Willie was reluctant, but left him, made it to Sweden and was repatriated. Willie never spoke of his exploits. He was such a good-natured fellow, and at Goldcrest he was in the regulating office, a kind of naval policeman.

There was a leading hand in the regulating office who was a right stroppy character. No one had any respect for him. He was probably frustrated because he couldn't get promotion to a higher rank, so took it out on those he thought were privileged. One day, Taffy and I were passing the office when he shouted to Taff: "Hey, you there, you're not properly dressed". Whereupon both Taff and I said: "We are". But then he said that Taff was not wearing the regulation naval jacket and collar; instead, poor Taff was wearing an army-type battledress jacket, navy blue in colour, which was the usual casual dress for aircrew. We tried to tell him that we were classed as aircrew, but he would have none of it. He told Taff to be back in ten minutes, properly dressed, or he would be on a charge. He knew that the photo section where we lived was three-quarters of a mile away, and he had no chance of making it back in time, even on a bike. The killick (leading hand) thought the result a foregone conclusion, and yelled "Get a move on, you're using up your time". We hastened round the corner and I said "Quick Taff – to the NAAFI". We were both about the same size, so we quickly changed clothing and I remained in the NAAFI while he dashed to the regulating office to report back. Just three minutes later he was back, laughing all over his face, for the stupid leading hand had no idea how he'd done it.

RATS, WRENS
AND WALRUSES

The section building where Taff and I lived was made of corrugated iron sheets and semi-circular in shape, like most of the other buildings at Dale. However, our place had an inner shell, made of what seemed to be compressed cardboard. This left a gap of about 3-4 inches between the sheets of iron and the cardboard, which led to a problem with rats. They got into the gap from the outside, and we could hear them scampering up the slope. We would bang on the board and listen as they slid down to the bottom. Occasionally, they gnawed their way through the board at the base, which gave them access to our living quarters. We tried to block off these holes with used-up photographic plates, as we reckoned that it was impervious to their teeth. But of course they just came through elsewhere. We tried to be crafty and electrocute them: we placed a glazed metal sheet on a bench, put two bricks on it, then another metal sheet on the bricks. We then put bait on the upper metal sheet and attached bare wires, one to each sheet. We hoped that a rat would put its rear paws on the lower sheet, its front paws on the top sheet, and thus be sped to rat heaven in the sky. We never had a single success, so we gave up on the idea. After that it was live and let live – until one night when I had obtained some sausages for breakfast the next morning, and left them on a bench in their wrapping. During the night I heard a scuffle. I switched on the light and saw a rat disappearing through the door with my sausage links. Taffy and I ran after it, only to see it dive into a large bin where we put our waste photographic paper. It could not get out because the sides were vertical, so we got a nearby fire hose and dropped the heavy brass nozzle into the bin repeatedly, until the scuffling ceased. On emptying the bin we found a big dead rat, but the sausages were no longer fit to eat. He did not get his meal, but neither did we.

The days were not without other incidents. One day, our petty officer, Fred Rodgers, took the station commander up in a Walrus amphibious biplane to do some photography. The commander's surname was Sholto Douglas; he was a relative of the RAF Air Vice Marshal. All went well until they came in to land, when they got a signal from the control tower that they should circle the airfield. There was a problem with their plane. A call went out for the emergency services to be on standby – the ambulance, fire tenders, and of course photographers to record all aspects of the expected accident. Taffy went to one section of the runway, I went to the other, and the aircraft came in with permission to land. As it approached, we could see that one of the tyres had split and the inner tube was oozing through the casing, looking like a big balloon. The Walruses did not have retractable undercarriages, so their wheels were clearly visible from the ground. After circling until given the all clear, with all the emergency services now in place, it came in and landed. Luckily, there was no problem, for the tyre did not blow out. When Fred climbed down and saw the cause of the bother, he fainted. Never a dull moment on photographic duty!

The Photographic Section at HMS Goldcrest in 1947: our four Wren film assessors, and the photographers (from left to right) Wynford 'Taffy' Williams, Petty Officer Fred Rodgers and Bob Walton

Sometime late in 1946, Taff and I were joined by four Wren assessors. They naturally lived in the Wrens' quarters. Their job was to assess cine films. We had some fighter aircraft on base, so when the pilots were being trained or needed further practice, the aircraft fitters would remove the guns from the wings of the aircraft. We then gave them cameras loaded with film, which were inserted where the guns had been. When the pilots were airborne and practising dogfights, a picture was taken whenever they pressed the gun buttons. We photographers then took the reels of film and developed them. The Wren assessors had the job of judging the skills of the pilots as recorded on film.

Each ship had its education officers, who were probably there to help the semi-literate ratings to improve themselves. We had an education section on Goldcrest with the attendant Lt schoolmaster. He decided to organise educational trips using naval vehicles on the occasional Sunday to such places as castles or ancient sites. I was always interested in such things, and so I went on these trips along with the four Wrens in our section. One day, we visited an old site that was remarkably like Stonehenge, but much smaller. It had an iron fence around it to protect it from sheep and cattle grazing in the fields. As we approached this relic, "Schoolie" went into his spiel about the site, then he said "I expect you are wondering how the ancient Brits managed to lift the stones over the fences". Whereupon I replied: "No sir, they brought them through the gate". I was not so popular with Schoolie that day, for I had spiked his punchline for this particular relic.

WORK ON THE SIDE

Photographic personnel had an advantage over other ratings in that they were permitted to run a business on the side that we called "The Firm". If an established photography firm wasn't in operation when we got a posting, then we would make out a price list, send it to the appropriate authority, and wait for the captain to apply his signature. If it was granted, as was generally the case, then we posted the price list up in the section entrance and waited for business to come through the door. There was one condition, however: we had to use our own materials, and do the work in our own time. I can't say we always followed the rules, though. Taff and I set up our own firm in Dale, doing such things as processing people's private films, taking portraits in our "studio", and so on. It must be remembered that many things were still scarce in this immediate post-war period, and getting films and having them processed was not an easy task. In any case, it could take a long time for such a job to be done on the outside. But we offered a quick, efficient service, even to the point of putting back naval requirements to satisfy our clientele. All proceeds from the firm were put into a kitty until we went on leave, when the share-out was made. It helped to give a boost to going on leave.

We did a considerable amount of naval work, of course – we were not just trying to earn extra cash. There was one incident I clearly remember, concerning a driver who was in the Royal Marines. He had been driving one of the large Navy wagons in Haverfordwest and was involved in an incident with a civilian driver. It was expected that he would be up on a charge for careless driving, since he was coming out of a minor road and should have given way at the junction. I was asked to photograph the scene of the accident. The same marine drove me to the junction, and I started to take the appropriate shots. The driver told me that he could not see any warning signs indicating who had right of way. So I climbed into the driving seat, opened the windscreen (it was on hinges), and proceeded to make a photographic record of the fact that nearby trees were obstructing the road signs. I also noted that the white lines on the road were virtually obliterated. Since this was just after the War, there were presumably priorities that were more important than road repairs. A driver would have been lucky to see the signs. I returned to base, processed the films, and passed them on to the authorities. Sometime later the marine came looking for me in the NAAFI full of praise and offering to buy me drinks in plenty. He had got off the charge as a result of my photographic evidence.

On one occasion, the Admiral (Air) paid us a visit. Instructions were given that photographers had to be in attendance to record all aspects of the event. It was a boon for "The Firm". We followed the admiral all over, taking his picture while he inspected and talked to the officers and personnel. The captain wanted a record of the visit for himself. We could not make a profit from him for the snaps we took, but any officer or rating who required a personal photo was charged accordingly. This visit provided me with an additional problem, because the admiral was also visiting a small airfield about 30 miles away where they had no photographer. I was instructed to hot-foot it there in a vehicle with a marine driver as soon as the admiral took off from Dale, so I could catch him on landing. We made it with seconds to spare and I followed him all over the airfield, in the hangars, the control tower, and wherever he made a stop to inspect things. The name of this small establishment was Brawdy.

The winter of 1946-47 was severe, and our airfield was in an exposed position on the Pembrokeshire coast. Once that winter, we were completely cut off by heavy falls of snow. The narrow roads leading to the base were blocked, and the captain ordered all personnel to help dig a way down to the beaches to allow landing craft to bring in essential supplies and the mail. There was one group that was excused such duties: the photographic section, because we were part of any emergency team, should any untoward incidents occur. Poor us! We just had to sit in our section hut playing cards, keeping warm by turning up the heaters and blowers in the film-drying rooms, while sympathising with the labouring ratings.

The role of naval photographer came back into my life more than 50 years after my demob. I was assigned to be host to the speaker at one of my Rotary Club's ladies evenings. I sat talking to the guest speaker (whom I knew since he was also a Rotarian, though he was a member at another club in the area). I asked him: "How are you finding retirement, Alan?" I knew he had finished work two years before. He said he was very busy and had just been to RAF Leeming, an air station not too far away. "I went to see the work of a Royal Air Force photographer, since it's one of my hobbies", he said. To which I replied: "How strange! I was a naval photographer in the nineteen forties". His interest was immediately obvious, and it was he who first asked if I could put something on paper about the life of a "snaps" in the early days.

Clearing a path to the photo section
with Taffy Williams in the winter of 1946-7

NAVAL THEATRICALS

The first few months of service life gave no opportunity for settling into any stage work, because every few weeks we would move on to different naval establishments to continue our training. I auditioned for a part in a straight play while in Felpham, though only three or four people were required and I was unsuccessful. The officer casting and directing the play was one Hedley Goodall, a professional actor who later had roles on TV up to the 1970s (incidentally, he was the first officer to have me punished in the Navy. He was the duty officer one night when I was doing guard duty at the Photography School, and I went for a cocoa break too soon in the early hours of the morning. Something must have upset him because he was in a foul mood).

It was after being posted to HMS Goldcrest in Pembrokeshire that I was able to continue my stage work. Some weeks after my arrival at the air base, auditions were held to form a concert party on the station. I auditioned and was accepted. Since this was immediately after the war, when conscription was still in force, there were men and women from all walks of life being drafted into service life, among them many fine performers. So I thought myself lucky to be successful. The party was called the "Goldcrest Goofers", and the shows consisted of comedy sketches, music and dancing, with Wrens providing the high-kicking chorus lines. Apart from on-ship shows, we went to other service establishments in the area such as the RAF flying boat base at Pembroke Dock, from where they flew Sunderland flying boats on Atlantic patrols. This concert party provided me with my first experience of working with a large company, for all my previous appearances (apart from school) had been as a solo performer. I found it most enjoyable. There was one act that sticks in my memory. There was a petty officer who in his novelty act ate razor blades and glass tumblers. At the end of his performance, when he came backstage, no one was allowed to enter his dressing room until he emerged afterwards. I went in once soon after him, and saw blood in the washbasin where he had been washing himself.

GETTING DEMOBBED

The time for my demob was drawing closer, and in the late summer of 1947 I was transferred back to my port division of Lee-on-Solent ready for the event. I arrived at Lee and each day looked in the Master-at-Arms office window for my demob number to appear (my number was 66). Then one day I spotted it. I knew that it was actually too early, but nevertheless I thought: "What the heck, my number is there, if they put it in the window, it's their fault not mine". So I reported for demob. Off we all went – the men correctly designated for demob, plus myself. Halfway through the demob routine, the door to the office opened and a chief petty officer came in. He shouted out my name and service number. "Out!" he said, "You're not due yet, return to your duties". So off I went, knowing it was at least six weeks before I would be legally due for discharge. What did I do? I applied for entry to an EVT course. This was an Educational Vocational Training course, specifically designed to prepare you for civvy street. I didn't know exactly what they had on these courses, so I opted to refresh my knowledge of chemistry. There was such a course available in Stafford in the midlands, so I joined it. It was just a month's skiving until my return to Daedalus, but I enjoyed it. We would go into Stafford on evenings to go to the pictures or to go dancing, the only drawback being that we had to get naval transport to the town and back. There was no public transport available. If we wanted to stay out late, there was no transport after 10 pm. We then had to take the late train from Stafford to Crewe, sleep on the station using the facilities provided for servicemen, then next morning board the early morning train heading north from Crewe. There was a stop near to the base where we would get out, then we would have to walk the half-mile to our base, arriving just in time for roll-call. There is always going to be someone who makes a hash of it. We once had a southerner who got the early morning train from Crewe but fell asleep. When he woke up, he asked someone in the compartment if the train had passed his station. They told him: "Yes, we stopped there five minutes ago". When they told him the next stop was Carlisle, he rushed out into the corridor, waited until he thought the train was going slower, then jumped out. He lost his hat, was slightly dazed, walked the wrong way for a while, then realised where he was and walked back to base. He was late for muster of course, had no hat, and was cut and bruised. He was charged with being late for duty, absent from his place of duty, being improperly dressed, and so on, and was punished accordingly.

At the end of this month I returned to Lee and to my demob. This time there was no hitch, but I made sure I was bubbly bosun that day – my last in the Navy, with my last Navy tot of Navy rum. As was the custom, I got sippers from my mess mates, then set off in the transport to be issued with my civilian clothes. This was a complete outfit, from head to toe. The demob centre for the Navy was somewhere in Fareham, I believe, but having been bubbly bosun, much of what went on that day was cloudy. I still can't remember the journey up from Pompey to London. I think I slept all the way. When I got home, my first act was to give my father the trilby hat I had been given, for I didn't like wearing hats at that time. It was years before I wore a hat again. So I was in civvy street once more. The one sad thing about my return was that my mother died just six months later, only a week or so after my 21st birthday in March 1948.

WORKING FOR
A LIVING AGAIN

After my short period on demob pay (three months), I had to find work and restart my life as a civilian. I was offered the chance to go to Germany with some agency or other to carry on with photographic work. Having been away from home for so long, I didn't wish to work abroad, so I turned it down. However, I was then given the chance to work in the research department at the ICI chemical works in Billingham, 20 miles south of Ryhope. The only problem was, it meant a daily trip there and back. I had no car, and in any case, cars weren't an everyday means of transport as they are today. Petrol was also still rationed, and such a daily journey to work would have eaten up my petrol ration. So, as I shall explain in greater detail below, I used to take the bus.

In 1948, however, I decided to get my driving licence. I took lessons from a chap in Sunderland who had a driving school, and I passed first time. I now decided I wanted to buy a car. But the post-war production of luxuries such as vehicles for the private motorist had not yet begun properly. Cars were scarce, new ones were virtually unobtainable, and so prices on the second-hand market were sky-high. My uncle Bill Duell offered to go round the garages with me, looking for a second-hand vehicle, for he had had cars for years and knew much more than I did about buying. However, Uncle Bill could not make find a satisfactory deal with any of the garages we visited, so there was no car for Robert.

Then Austin announced they were bringing out a new type of car. It was to be in two models: the Devon and the Dorset saloon. One was a four-door model, while the other had two doors. Because of the shortage of cars, the government decreed that anyone who bought a new car could not sell it until eighteen months after purchase. The idea was to prevent people buying new vehicles, then exploiting the bottleneck between supply and demand by selling them at a massive profit. There were plenty of racketeers back then, particularly in the car market.

When Austin announced their new cars, I went to Binn's garage in Sunderland and ordered a two-door Dorset saloon. I still had my gratuity (the sum of money given to all servicemen on demobilisation) and also had a steady job, so I believed I could afford it. I filled in the paper work, got the whole speech from the salesman, and was told it would be delivered in about eighteen months. I'm still waiting for it, more than 50 years later. That shows a fair degree of patience on my part, does it not?

I worked on a variety of tasks at the research department of ICI, from routine analysis and synthesis to pure research, making compounds that no one had made before. This work was not without its dangers, however. One colleague nearly lost his sight when there was an explosion in the lab. I believe he had unknowingly created a fulminate, not a particularly stable substance. I once had a glass flask explode in my hand while working in a fume cupboard. Luckily, I was wearing protective clothing and thick gloves on my hands, though my left hand was red and sore for hours afterwards. Sometime before this, I had a bad cough. So I went to my doctor, who asked: "Have you been working with chlorine?" – to which I replied: "Yes". He knew my trouble straightaway. Once, we were trying to find a fertiliser that could allow farmers to obtain two crops per year instead of one. This work was based on a class of compounds called gibberellins. Since we didn't know the possible effects of such new compounds, we had to go the medical centre at least twice a year for a complete check-up.

Working for such a large company as ICI, you had the opportunity to do a great variety of work. So eventually, in order to broaden my scope in the chemical field, I asked for a change and was sent "down the yard". This was a term for working on the actual manufacturing side of the business. I remained on that side of the industry for the rest of my time with the company. At first I was the site water economy officer. It was feared that demand for water, which was such an important raw material, would exceed supply over the coming years. So it was vital to plan ahead. My job after this was being in charge of the site distribution of water, gas, nitrogen, compressed air and so on. In 1977, I felt that another change was needed, as I seemed to be getting into a rut with my job. So I asked for a transfer. It was granted, and I finished off my last few years working for the company doing water chemistry as the assistant to my friend Dr David Lester. Working with David involved much travelling, not only to many parts of the UK, but also to Canada and Europe. This last appointment was just about the most enjoyable and satisfying work I did whilst with ICI. Not just because of the people I worked with, but also because we were recognised specialists in our field.

ICI Billingham, 1970 (photo by Ben Brooksbank,
https://commons.wikimedia.org/w/index.php?curid=26367680)

TRAVELLING IN TRIUMPH

Many people travelled from Sunderland, Ryhope, Seaham or Easington to work in Billingham just after the war. Since not many folk had cars, public transport was still the best way to get to and from your workplace. There were two ways of getting to Billingham: by train or by bus. The train was not entirely satisfactory, because the timetable did not fit in well with normal working hours (though it was better for those working shifts). Only a small number of workers took the train; most took the bus, as did I. The bus company that ran services from Sunderland to Middlesbrough was called "The Triumph Bus Co.". There were two services, direct and indirect. After Easington, the direct service went through Old Shotton and Castle Eden, then on to Wolviston, Billingham and Stockton before ending in Middlesbrough. The indirect service turned off to Shotton Colliery after Easington, travelling on through Wheatley Hill, Wingate, Hutton Henry, and then at the Hutton Henry Lane it met the A19, taking up the direct route to Middlesbrough. Being regular travellers, it was economical to purchase a three-month or six-month pass. Not only was it cheaper, but you then didn't have to bother with keeping change to buy the daily return tickets. And a pass could be used at any time.

The buses left Sunderland at different times. The one we used most was the direct service, leaving the town at 7 am. I joined it at Ryhope at 7:10 am, and it arrived in Billingham at about 8:20 am, just in time for an 8:30 start. The indirect bus left 30 mins or so before the other service, but it was useful if you had to start work earlier for some reason. To return in the evening, we would board the bus that left Stockton at 5:10 pm, this being a direct bus. The pick-up point was Billingham Green, where it was due at 5:20 pm. Once again, the timing was perfect for a 5:00 pm finish at work. There were problems, however, particularly in the summer when people flocked to Stockton market on Wednesday afternoons. This resulted in the busses having to cope not just with the regular workers, but also with day-trippers. So when we tried to get on at Billingham Green, the bus was often full. It must be remembered that there was only one bus per hour. The solution to our problem was to get one of the many works buses outside the offices. These went to Hartlepool, but we could get off at Wolviston. By the time the Triumph bus got to Wolviston, some of its irregular passengers would have disembarked already, which meant we could get on board and continue with our journey home. This trick usually worked, but not always. On rare occasions, we had to travel on to Hartlepool and get a United bus from there to Ryhope. This meant a very long working day.

Regular passengers got to know the bus crews, and they us, and this paid dividends on many an occasion. One day, I was waiting at the bus stop in Wolviston High Street. When it arrived it was full to the brim, but there were about six or seven people waiting to board, only three of us regular passengers. The concertina door of the bus jerked open, then the conductress popped her head out, and said: "I want only three: him, him, and him" – she was pointing to us regulars. We didn't argue, but just jumped aboard. She shut the door quickly, and the bus was off before the other people realised what had happened.

One day, the bus came in from Stockton, but went straight past the stop at the Green. It must have had more than the usual number of workers from town. However, I knew that the bus was often delayed at the level crossing near the railway station. So I ran the half-mile like mad. As I approached the station, I saw the bus standing at the gates waiting for the train to pass. I dashed past the bus, ran up the steps of the bridge and over the lines, then down the other side, and got to the bus stop just as the gates opened. One person got off, and I got on.

Knowing which passengers got on at what stop meant that the bus crews knew who would be waiting at the various stops along the way. On the very rare occasions when I was a trifle late, they would wait for me to arrive. One day I was a minute or two behind time. I crossed the road as the bus was approaching, waved at it, but it went on round the corner all the same. Thinking they had not seen me, I ran round the corner, and the bus was waiting there. "Didn't you see me waving?", I asked. "Yes", said the driver. "But we thought you could do with the exercise".

This familiarity with the bus crews had its embarrassing side, such as when I was going from Ryhope to Sunderland. My pass wasn't valid for this journey, but if I got on a Triumph bus and the staff on it knew me, they would say: "Oh, you have a pass", and charge me nothing. It was no good telling them that the pass was only from Ryhope to Billingham, not in the opposite direction, from Ryhope to Sunderland. They just ignored my pleas, even when I offered them the fare. And the bus inspectors who occasionally got on to check our tickets were no different. On a number of occasions I forgot my pass when going to work, but the inspector would walk up the aisle, checking the tickets of the other passengers, but just saying hello to me as he passed. The inspectors would often even come and sit beside me to have a chat.

One summer evening, I was going to the pictures in Stockton with pals from work. I intended to get the 9 pm bus back from Stockton High Street, at the stop outside what is now Spencer Hall Market. The bus was due to come from Middlesbrough, over the Victoria Bridge up into Stockton High Street. It would then make a U-turn just beyond the Town Hall, then halt at the stop, facing the same direction from which it had come. After a few minutes rest for the crew, the bus would then go back down the street, do another U-turn at the crossroads near the Odeon, then carry on to Norton and Billingham. This evening, I left the cinema and stood waiting with a number of other passengers for the bus to arrive. It came in, did its U-turn, but when it came to the stop I saw it was full. What a pickle! I couldn't jump the queue, but went to the front of the bus where the two crew members were standing. The driver said: "Go across the road to the Odeon, Bob, and wait". This I did. And when they set off, they performed their U-turn, the bus slowed down outside the cinema, the door opened, and I jumped on. Saved by a friendly crew.

There were always odd characters travelling on the bus, and people from all walks of life. We had one regular passenger who worked at the hide and skin yard somewhere in Stockton. In the summer weather when the temperature was up, we certainly knew it if he got on the bus! During the War, there was a prisoner-of-war camp a mile or two north of Wolviston. It had been vacated, of course, and squatters had moved into the huts on the site. Housing was in such short supply that squatting was a frequent occurrence. Many of these squatters worked in Billingham or Stockton, and the bus company made the camp one of its regular stops. This hide-and-skin worker was one of them. There was also a couple who were squatters, and who both worked at ICI. So I knew them by sight, but they gave the impression that they didn't wish people to know where they lived. So they used to get off the bus at a stop a couple of hundred yards further on from the former POW camp (though in fact everyone knew where they lived).

As I mentioned earlier, we regulars bought passes lasting three or six months. There was one chap who lived in the village of Hutton Henry along the indirect bus route, which lay about a mile from the point where the village road met the A19. He had discovered that it was cheaper to buy his pass to run from the lane end instead of from Hutton Henry. So for a few coppers he would then purchase an extra ticket that covered the stretch down to the A19 stop. However, there was a peculiar aspect to this. If anyone was already at the A19 stop when the bus arrived, this man had to get off the bus, let the other person or persons on, and then get back on himself. This was because, technically speaking, his journey was complete, for he had bought a ticket up to that point. From that stop onwards, his pass was valid. The strange situation did not end there. Because if no one was at the stop, the bus still came to a halt. The man would step off the bus, on to the ground, and the conductress would hold the door open while he turned round and remounted the steps to board the bus again and go back to his seat. We never found out why this was important, but someone in the company offices must have decreed that the man in question was in breach of some regulation or other if he did not get off. What would we make of such a strange situation today?

In the 1950s, the A19 was not a dual carriageway as it is today. It twisted and turned all the way, except for a short stretch between Easington and Old Shotton. It could be a difficult road for any driver in the winter, what with the risk of frost, ice and fog. One winter's morning, there was a covering of black ice on the road surface. As we drove past the stop outside the Red Lion pub at Dalton Piercy, the bus slowly drove down the incline, but the driver lost control on the ice, the bus spun round and came to a stop across the road, blocking it in both directions. What could he do? With a busload of passengers he had plenty of help to call on. He shouted: "OK boys, can you push me back on track?" We all piled out of the bus and pushed and shoved till the old vehicle was back facing south again, and off we went once more. No call for roadside assistance was necessary. In fact, this wasn't the first time we had had to push a bus. If the engine stalled at a stop – which happened now and then – then we would all get out to push and help him on his way. On these occasions, however, he had to keep the engine running, driving the bus slowly along while we ran like mad to get back on board.

On another dark winter's morning on the A19, there was a very thick fog. We were approaching Elwick lane ends, and the driver was going carefully because of the conditions. Then the bus came to a halt, the conductress opened the door, looked out, saw no one waiting outside, and so gave the driver two rings of the bell (which was the signal to go). The sliding glass panel behind the driver opened, and he shouted: "You silly girl, Annie!" – or words to that effect – "we're in a field". Sure enough, there was a nasty bend in the road at the lane end, and in the thick fog the driver had missed the bend, driving straight ahead through an open gate into a field before realising what he'd done, at which he had stopped the bus. Once more, the passengers came to the rescue by guiding him backwards out of the gate and on to the road again. Poor Annie had thought it was the Elwick Lane bus stop.

This familiarity didn't just go one way. One evening, I had to work late and caught a late bus back from Billingham. This bus was manned by one of the Sunderland crews, and the conductress was a girl called June Croft. When we were some distance along the road, a chap boarded the bus, and it was obvious that June knew him. There was hardly anyone else on the bus. So after a while, she said to me: "Bob, will you look after the front of the bus for me?" Naturally I said "Yes". She immediately went to the rear of the bus with her chap and started canoodling. It meant that Bob stood there, opening and closing the door, letting people on and off the bus while she was with her boyfriend on the back seat of the vehicle.

Earlier on, I mentioned my first teacher at infant school, Miss Smith. I never thought that many years later her husband would enter my life in a strange way. I was returning from work one summer evening, just sitting and enjoying the view of the countryside. The bus had just left Old Shotton. We were approaching Peterlee lane ends, when I heard a sound to my right. I looked in the direction of the sound and there, crawling along the window ledge, was a snake. I didn't panic, but got up from my seat and went down to the front of the bus to tell the conductress: "Peggy, have you one of those shovels you carry in the bus during the winter?" She replied "No Bob, why?" I told her about the snake, but naturally she thought I was joking. Then suddenly there was a scream further up the bus, and we saw the snake wriggling down the centre aisle – it was one of those aisles that were below the level of the seats.

People were standing up in disbelief. They could not imagine a snake would be on a public vehicle, as such things are just not encountered in England. But there was one chap, an RAF sergeant with a big build, who rose from his seat, placed one hand on the back of each seat on either side of the aisle, raised both feet from the floor, and dropped his size-ten boots on top of the snake as it slithered beneath him. Goodbye, snake. The sergeant picked the snake up by the tail, walked to the front of the bus, Peggy opened the door, and he threw the beast out.

This RAF man was the husband of Miss Smith. Life can be funny at times.

At the funfair, Seaburn, Whitsun 1948.
From left: Aaron Ridley, Bess Lilley, Bob and Alan Yeaman

Seaburn, Whitsun 1948.
From left: Aaron Ridley, John Curtis (a colleague from Bess's office), Bob

Bob at Stanley Park in Blackpool, July 1949

With Bess at the Festival of Britain, London, 1951

POST TRIUMPH

It was in the late 1940s after my demob that I started courting Bessie Lilley. We got married on 9 February 1952. King George VI died that same week, so everything had a subdued atmosphere. The television was in its early days, with everything in black and white, but all normal programmes were cancelled anyway. All we saw were still pictures on the screen and the sound of Sandy Macpherson playing organ music in the background.

It was a year after our wedding that we made our first trip to Switzerland. Little did we think that, many years later, we would be making regular journeys there to visit our son, his wife and our grandchildren in Zurich. It was not long after our first Swiss trip that I acquired my first car: a 10 hp Singer Super 10. It had been built in 1947, so it was of pre-War specifications. That meant thick gauge metal in its construction, real leather upholstery, a heater (which was just an electric element hanging below the dashboard), and of course a clock (which never really worked). The boot lid opened downwards and there was very little room for luggage in the back, since most of the space was taken up by the spare wheel. The car did have a sun roof – which was quite a luxury – as well as an extremely useful feature for driving in foggy weather, namely a windscreen that opened upwards when you turned a handle on top of the dashboard. The bonnet was in two sections, so when one wanted to inspect the engine you had to lift up each side in turn. This car always had mechanical problems, but it brought me independent mobility, and gave Bess and me much pleasure.

There were a number of us from Ryhope and Seaham who worked at ICI, so we formed a travelling club. This cut the cost of the journey quite considerably, but also naturally meant that my years with the Triumph Bus Co. and its crews came to an end. It was my car that we used most often to travel to ICI. I would first pick up a chap called Eddie Brewer who lived near me. Then we drove on to Seaham to pick up Harold, and afterwards picked up the last member of our club, who lived at Peterlee. If I had car trouble, then Harold would drive us in his Ford. One morning, Eddie and I were quite early in getting to Seaham and Harold was not at the pick-up point. So we drove down the road to where he lived. His was a terraced house with a front path but no road, so we had to go round the back street to park. We stopped at what we thought was his rear door, banged loudly on it and shouted for Harold, calling out that he was a lazy devil. Then Eddie said: "There he is, at the top of the street". I reversed the car and stopped near him. When he got in the car, we told him where we had been. It turned out we had been to the wrong house. So we didn't hang around there too long.

I had just as many unusual incidents with this car as I'd had on the Triumph buses. One day, I was near Easington village with my passengers. We had just passed the dog track, I turned a bend in the road, and suddenly had to brake sharply. Before us was something I never had seen before or since: an elephant with its minder straight ahead of us, stomping slowly along and its tail flapping to and fro. We all gaped in disbelief: an elephant, walking along the road outside Easington at 8 am in the morning. Apparently there was a touring circus in the area that was moving site. The larger animals – such as the one we saw – were generally walked to the next venue if it was not too far away, and in such cases – as here – they would leave early on a morning before any traffic built up. The rest of their company, with all their equipment and the smaller animals, would follow on by rail or road.

In those days there was no A19 by-pass road for Easington, and today's road layout is quite different in the village itself. As you left Easington, there was a large green area where the road from Hetton to Horden crossed the old A19. One winter's morning, the roads were slippery with black ice where the road sloped down from Hetton. Suddenly, a small wagon appeared down the slope, with its passenger waving to us. I straightaway knew what the problem was: he couldn't stop on the icy surface. I was on the major road and naturally had priority, but I slowed down to let him cross my path, then saw him safely negotiate the bend at the bottom of the slope before he carried on along the road to Horden. I can still see him, waving and looking scared.

THE SYNTHONIA PLAYERS

It was a short while after I started working at the ICI laboratories that I met two men who would have a considerable impact on my future work for the amateur stage. They were Stan Burnicle – an organist, pianist, raconteur and player of the penny-whistle – and Ken Hodgson, who was an exceedingly talented pianist and lyricist. They must have overheard me in conversation one day when I mentioned that I had worked in a concert party in the Navy. So they asked if I would join them in a musical sketch for a section party. I agreed, and this was the beginning of many years of performing at many different venues, most particularly with Stan Burnicle.

That small section party led to the annual departmental party and an invitation to join the "Synthonia Players", an amateur theatre group attached to the ICI recreational club. The Research departmental party was an annual event eagerly awaited by all concerned.

It took place in the Synthonia Theatre on the ICI site in Billingham. Anything up to 200 people attended these shows. The participants spent weeks in rehearsal. Well-known songs would be sung, but with their words rewritten to express a gripe at a company policy, to voice a complaint humorously, or to have a joke at the expense of some person well-known in the department. When you consider that the department employed chemists, physicists, mathematicians and linguists who had studied at major universities in the UK, Europe and beyond, it perhaps isn't surprising that there was also a wealth of talented scriptwriters, lyricists and musicians among them.

Here's a verse from a Research party show to illustrate how a grievance could be communicated – in this instance, the fact that New Year's Day was not recognised by ICI as a public holiday back at the time (in the 1950s):

I regret my recent absence from employment
On the day of Tuesday January 1st,
When a sudden insurrection
By a virusoid infection
Caused an introverted follicle to burst.
With a pain in my aurora borealis
And a pulmonary lung I've always had,
I was led to my physician
With acute indisposition.
In other words: I was bad.

It was while we were preparing for one of these Research parties that Stan suggested we might introduce a mock ventriloquist act into the party. Since both Stan and Ken were six feet tall, it was obvious who they thought should be the dummy. A script was prepared, and the first time we did it, Ken was the "human" to my dummy, but after that, Stan took on his role, which also meant carrying me onto the stage. The act was an immediate hit, so we repeated it the following year and the year after that. Stan and I formed such a good partnership that we kept repeating this vent act for almost 25 years at assorted venues in the area.

In 1965 I was awarded an "Oscar" by the organising committee in recognition of my work over the years as performer, lyricist, and writer of monologues – it was a glass statuette made by the departmental glassblowers and based on the one from Hollywood. I held it for one year and then passed it on to the next recipient.

1965 was also the year when I moved from the Research Department. It was at my own request, for I had a desire to become more involved with the production side of chemical manufacturing. I did continue to appear in the Research parties for a while as a guest performer, though. As time went on I became involved in "Works" functions as a performer, scriptwriter and organiser. There were retirement affairs, smokers, and Works social events. After about ten years, however, this came to an end when I moved to yet another new job on site. This post meant travelling quite a lot on company business, so it became impractical to continue any involvement in Works functions.

I mentioned before that I had become a member of the Synthonia Players. In 1961, it was proposed that we should put on a pantomime. It was a large production, and was staged in January 1962 at the Synthonia Theatre. "Aladdin" was chosen as the topic. The script and music were all original, and it was the first panto to be staged in the theatre since before the War – it had been damaged during a bombing raid and had only recently been repaired.

Aladdin was the first of several pantos that the Synthonia Players produced. We played to nearly full houses for six nights, with a matinee on the Saturday afternoon. It was a novel event for the area, so the press attended in force. I hadn't realised that they were going to be present, so I was surprised when I met Ken in the corridor the next day and he told me about the reviews. On 17 January 1962, "LC" wrote in the Northern Echo:

> I found myself writing "too subdued" against many of the names on my programme. Two who escaped this treatment, however, were Rita Lightfoot and Bob Walton (Genies of the ring and lamp respectively). They captured the atmosphere of the show and, what is more, succeeded in projecting it to the audience.

And "K. McG." wrote in the Billingham Express:

> … the two characters one warmed to most were Rita Lightfoot (Genie of the Ring) and Bob Walton (Genie of the Lamp). Their brushes with the villain, Abanaza (Ken Bett) and his two browbeaten henchmen Abdul and Mustaphar (Frank Brown and Ken Thwaite) were hilarious.

The next two years saw further successes with Jack and the Beanstalk and Cinderella, again with favourable press reports.

These productions proved so popular that the Works social committees made block bookings for their annual children's outings instead of taking them to the professional productions with their big box-office names at the Stockton theatres.

These were the only three pantos that we performed in the Synthonia Theatre before moving on to other things. Our next theatrical effort was a revue – a series of musical and comedy sketches. However, I did participate in one more panto a year or so later. I had been invited to join a cast to stage Jack and the Beanstalk again, using our original script. Many of those taking part were members of the Synthonia Players, and the backstage helpers were also from the original production. The rehearsals were held in St Luke's Church at Low Grange in Billingham, and the panto was staged at Northfield School for two or three performances. But it was not up to the same standard as back at the Synthonia Theatre, mainly because of the lack of facilities and back-up assistance. The Synthonia Theatre was better equipped than many professional theatres in the provinces. There were backstage dressing rooms both upstairs and down, while there was a bar at the rear of the hall, above which was the dress circle, with the projection box situated behind it. We had a range of skilled craftsmen to assist with all our productions – electricians for lighting, joiners for making the sets, costume-makers, make-up artists and so on. We had front-of-house people, usherettes, and people to man the box office. Skilled operators were employed in the projection box to control the spots and the on-stage lighting. Musicians were available to accompany the performers and to give background continuity throughout the show. These large-scale shows entailed a considerable strain for an amateur company, when one bears in mind that preparations had to start months in advance of any show. And, as with any group of amateurs, there were other things to consider, such as the responsibilities of work, family and social life.

In the late 1960s, the Synthonia Players decided to stage an old-time music hall. It was intended to be similar to those that were broadcast from the City of Variety at Leeds, along with a gavel-wielding chairman. It was produced and directed by Stan Burnicle. The audience was encouraged to come in Victorian costume to give more flavour to the show. It played to packed houses for four nights, and a good time was had by all. One thing from this first music hall remains in my memory. On the posters advertising the show I was billed as:

Bob Walton
A Song, a Joke and a Rissole.

I asked Stan: "What's this about the rissole?" He replied: "Well, it made you laugh, didn't it? It might encourage more people to buy tickets, just to find out what it's all about".

I still have that poster today.

Synthonia Theatre,
March 1969

Round Table Chairmen and their wives, greeting the new District Chairman for 1963-64. Bess and Bob Walton, third and fourth from right

Newly installed President of Billingham Rotary Club in 1983, with Bess, the outgoing President Bill Prediger, and his wife Enid

After the success of this music hall, we decided to put on a follow-up show the next year. This time, we ran for five nights. The posters advertised "Comedy, melodrama, ballads, and popular chorus numbers". Although we did not know it at the time, this production was to be the last of the Synthonia Players. The precise reasons are obscure, but it may have been because of changes in Company policy regarding the recreation club. Some members of the players suggested breaking away from the Synthonia Club. An extraordinary general meeting was called, at which a majority favoured severing our ties. They also decided to rename themselves "The Billingham Players" and to take up residence in the Co-op buildings near Billingham Green. Their new venue in the hall above the Co-op became known as "The Theatre Upstairs". These amateur players are still going strong, but tend to concentrate on serious drama, whereas we had preferred a more humorous slant. Some of us – me, Stan, Ken and one or two others – voted not to change. We didn't wish to dissociate entirely from the club and from ICI. It was mainly the younger members who were keen to move on and start something new. Perhaps the club section was their best way of becoming involved in amateur theatre, whereas those of us who remained had other outlets too. Besides, we could not afford the time and effort needed to start something new. As far as I was concerned, I still had my Works functions to keep me occupied. I was also involved in other areas, such as fundraising events at my church, private parties and the like. I also had requests from various people for my services as a compère.

The main dread of any performer, I suppose, is drying up. It only ever happened to me twice, as I recall, and on both occasions it was in the Synthonia Theatre. The first took place during a Research party in front of about 200 people. I was doing a humorous song with Ken Hodgson on the piano, and I had a quartet as my backing group. We'd completed two verses when I turned to face the quartet as they sang the chorus. For some reason my mind went blank. I couldn't think of the opening line of the next verse. I whispered to the quartet "I've forgotten my lines, what's the start of the next verse?" No one could remember, and they had enough to do to remember their own words. I walked to the microphone, trying to think of the next verse, and then Ken played the opening chord for me to proceed. I turned to look at him; he played it again; and I said something such as "stop banging on the keyboard, I'm thinking". He looked at me and said: "You've forgotten the next verse, haven't you?" I replied: "Of course I have". He stood up from the piano, rustled some sheets on the top of the grand, selected one, walked towards me, placed his arm around my shoulder and said to the audience: "He may be forgetful, but he's a darn good chemist". Then he pushed the paper into my hand and said: "You won't forget now. There's the script". With measured strides and a final wink he calmly returned to sit at the piano, played the chord and we carried on as if nothing had gone wrong. My memory lapse had passed, and my confidence returned. After the show I was talking to some of the audience and realised that they didn't know I'd made a mistake. They'd thought that the hesitation and banter were all part of the act. One person actually said to me: "You chaps must have rehearsed well to get the timing and the repartee correct". I had no reason to shatter his illusions.

The second mistake was not actually drying up – it was sheer forgetfulness. It occurred during our vent act. Stan often had a table in front of us, and would sometimes tape the script to it as his prompt. I couldn't read the script while seated on his knee as the dummy. We were well into the act when he paused, looked at me, then looked at the audience, and shouted to them: "He's missed out at least half a page of script". He wasn't someone to panic. I suddenly realised what I'd done, so I swivelled my head in dummy fashion, and said: "Well, who's the one doing all the talking here?" I then swivelled my head back to face the audience, keeping a straight face, and heard the people out front falling over themselves with laughter. The situation was saved and we finished the act. When the curtains closed and we were walking back into the wings, Stan said "What an ad lib, we'll put that in the script for next time!" We did, and kept it for many years afterwards.

THE BILLINGHAM
INTERNATIONAL
FOLKLORE FESTIVAL

In the mid-1960s I was a member of Billingham Round Table when we were approached by the chairman of the committee organising the Billingham International Folklore Festival. He told us that the committee wanted to set up a kind of nightclub where the performers could relax after their concerts, and where the public could meet the artistes who came from the four corners of the globe. This Festival Club was to be held every night in the Billingham Arms Hotel for the duration of the Festival. Round Table was asked to help because they'd taken part in a similar venture in Middlesbrough, during the Eisteddfod that was held there. They thought it was an ideal enterprise for the Festival in Billingham too. Round Table agreed, and I was delegated to be the compère for the event, presumably because of my associations with the stage. I continued doing the job at the Festival for the next twenty years, until the Festival Club was discontinued because of failing support. At this point, the Festival director approached me to ask if I would continue my support by helping out as a stage announcer at the concerts in the Festival proper. These were held each afternoon in the open air in Billingham Town Centre, and then at the College Theatre in the evening. This was in about 1985, and I performed this task for the next 16 years, when I considered myself too old to be jumping on and off stage. By then I had reached the age of 74. It was at this point that I finally decided to retire altogether from active stage work.

NORTON HALL

Norton Hall, situated on Norton Green, was the social, sports and recreational club for ICI management. It had many sections that catered for all tastes, ranging from squash to croquet, photography, wine and music. In the late 1970s I was asked to join the committee of the music section, of which Stan Burnicle was chairman. Once a month, the music section organised a concert or lecture by people well-known in the world of music. Bookings were made either through a theatrical agency or through personal contacts. It was the duty of the committee to arrange a concert during the Christmas period each year. These concerts were repeated over two or three nights and were extremely well supported. I was also active in the concerts as a member of Stan's party. At the start of the 1990s, Stan and Ken alternated in arranging these concerts, for which each of them assembled his own collection of singers and musicians (though Ken was not actually a member of the committee). Stan and his party became the sole providers of the entertainment from about 1995 to 2001, when Norton Hall was sold off on account of the restructuring of ICI, and the club ceased to exist altogether.

When I retired from ICI in 1984, all my connections with its sections and social committees ended. The Research party had come to an end, while the Synthonia Players had left the scene some years before, as explained above. But I did not put up my feet and become an idle pensioner. The music section at Norton Hall was still going strong at the time, and that kept me busy. I was also receiving more and more requests to be an after-lunch or after-dinner speaker. I gave quite a number of talks, not only at my own Rotary Club and at others in the area, but also occasionally to other social groups on Teesside. My topics were varied, ranging from my experiences in the Navy to holidays and so on.

Stan Burnicle also formed his own small concert party away

from Norton Hall, and now and then he would ask me to help out with a monologue, a comedy song or such like if he had a booking in the area. These requests became more frequent over the years. He would ask: "Oh, Bob, can you do a five-minute spot here, and two minutes there?" Before long, I was a member of his group, and doing more than I had originally anticipated. As a result of this, I started to develop an act of my own. I would introduce myself and give a brief, fictional history of my life, though it was really just an opportunity to make it into a humorous saga with corny gags (such as "I was a war baby – my parents began to fight as soon as I was born"). The tale would then move on to my school, service life, and marriage. I also started to employ North East dialect in the act, and use it to develop humorous situations. We played in quite a number of venues in the area, including in Durham city.

All this came to an end, however when Stan suffered a stroke in 2002 and was unable to continue his concert work. The hardest part of the illness for him was not being able to play his piano or his electric organ. When his wife could no longer cope with him at home, he went into a nursing home. He still took his organ with him, in the hope that his fingers would at some time be able to work again. I visited him on a number of occasions. On the wall board in his room, where get-well cards were posted, I was pleased to see he also had a photograph of the two of us on stage, doing our vent act. He passed away within about a year, at which I lost a lot of my enthusiasm for the work. And anyway, I thought that one should consider bringing such things to a close when well into one's seventies. That was also about the time that I ceased helping out at the Folklore Festival, as I mentioned earlier.

I never expected or accepted any monetary payment for my theatrical work, since I looked upon it as pleasure, just as others enjoy their own hobbies or outdoor pursuits. However, I did receive payment for one concert with Stan. He had asked me to help with a fundraising venture for the church where he was the organist and choirmaster. I did so, and at tea and biscuits after the show, a lady member of the organising committee gave me an envelope that I assumed contained a thank-you card. On reaching home, however, I opened it to find £20 inside. I was flabbergasted, and returned the money the next day via Stan. The concert had been intended to raise much-needed funds for their church, so I couldn't keep it. This was the only time I can ever recollect having been paid.

I have almost come to the end of this walk down memory lane, except for mentioning the birth of our two children, Kathryn in 1957, and Christopher in 1963. I have not been able to put all my activities in strict chronological order because so many events overlapped. When one tries to recollect events taking place over so many years it is not easy to remember everything with a high degree of accuracy. My final word is that throughout this long period of my life on the stage I enjoyed doing something that was denied to many people. I would not have wanted it any other way. And I hope that my old elocution teacher, Miss Eales, wherever she is, will look down, smile, and say: "Bobby, you learnt your lessons well. They were worth it, were they not?"

INDEX